Digital

DIGITAL MARKETING

Certified

ABOUT THE AUTHOR

Ola "Tux" Abitogun is the Creator of…

myEmpirePRO.com – a media, publishing, consulting, and training company with digital marketing, electronic medical records, project management, and other related services. He became a FULL-TIME entrepreneur in October 2006.

He is a computer engineer and an engineering management graduate from the New Jersey Institute of Technology; (NJIT) class of 2004/5. He was born in Dallas, Texas, and raised in Nigeria by his Nigerian parents. He considers himself a proud Nigerian American.

Today, he is a marketing addict, trainer, marketing and business consultant, and all-around serial entrepreneur.

Digital Marketing Certified

Insider secrets to getting more traffic, leads, deals, customers, and clients and generating more income & revenue in a digital era.

OLA TUX ABITOGUN

TERMS OF USE

You can get your own copy at

www.DigitalMarketingCertified.com

ACKNOWLEDGEMENTS

To my beautiful wife and my kids, I love you forever. Thanks to my parents and extended family for doing an awesome job raising me. It's true. It takes a village. Thanks to all the numerous coaches and mentors over the years. Thanks to all the friends and family that have supported our family in prayer over the years. God bless you and your family. To God be all the glory.

Table of Content

THE INTRODUCTION

2009, February. This story was launched into new dimensions. A partner and friend invited me to a home meeting designed to launch a home business. I want to tell you that story but let's talk about this being my 4th published book for context.

Previously in the world of my book writing endeavors, I published my 3rd book called Real Estate Money Secrets (www.RealEstateMoneySecrets.com) as a follow-up to the first book I ever published called Smart Real Estate Wholesaling. (www.SmartRealEstateWholesaling.com)

Between those two books, I co-authored a book with my wife called Get My Marriage Back (www.GetMyMarriageBack.com) to help couples going through a crisis in marriage rekindle things in a sustainable and healthy way.

It is with great pleasure that I present to you my 4th published book, Digital Marketing Certified. I believe it will be my greatest work thus far toward my ongoing effort to continue putting more value out into the world.

Not just because it's going to help me make more money but honestly because it will help you add more value to the world, create a positive impact, and, yes, make more money.

It almost feels like my books are tracking my personal journey, which I am about to share with you in a second. I like it because it's starting to make sense.

There were times that I had planned to write other books in the past few years, but it just never happened. This book is not just written; you are also here reading it, and to me, that's a sign of lots of greatness that will come through you into this world.

Reading this book 10-15 times is not just about reading a book. It's about mastery of what it's going to take to connect your message and the value you have to offer the world with your core audience, literally millions of them waiting to receive your awesomeness.

I want to be able to track your progress and especially your story, as it's also being documented as you implement what you learn in this book; that's my greatest wish.

So 2009, February, as I was saying earlier, my digital marketing story was officially launched into new dimensions. A partner and a friend invited me into a home meeting designed to launch a home business in his apartment in West New York, New Jersey.

A multi-million dollar real estate business had just gotten wiped out from underneath me due to the 2008 recession. So I was open to ways of pivoting because I experienced massive unfathomable success between the ages of 26 and 28 years old.

You couldn't tell me anything. I was on top of the world, and suddenly, it was over. I tried building an online mall, a car export business, and a few other things. I just knew that I was never going into the 9-5 world.

I just always knew that I had more value in myself to offer the world. It feels like a whole big ball of fire inside of me, and it would be the greatest form of punishment to lock me inside of a cubicle for eight plus hours and 5 days per week or more.

In hindsight, I now know that I was naive and too young to be able to comprehend everything I have now learned since then, over 12 years.

Anyway, I ended up signing up for a network marketing business opportunity, and that officially launched me into the world of marketing.

With my prior real estate business, I leveraged the internet's power with direct response and email marketing in so many creative ways. But I didn't realize it was all digital marketing.

I recruited my whole family into the network marketing, multi-level marketing, and MLM business model, but they all did nothing with the business opportunity. So I received a $12 check months later in exchange for the $2,000 that I spent on signing them all up.

In 2014, I made my way back into real estate in collaboration with other investors, wholesaling, training, and coaching investors on how to market using my systems. But since 2009, there is one aspect of all these that I wake up to daily; that's marketing, and I am obsessed.

One of the most difficult and *"easy to be distracted from"* lessons I've discovered is that everyone needs a link to opportunities to serve. Let me explain.

We all want not just to survive but we want to be financially stable enough to enjoy the things we like to enjoy. Let's just address the elephant in the room.

We all want more money, no matter how much we already have. Everytime you get a raise in income, and a new problem is created. Naturally, the cost of your lifestyle follows suit.

There is not much difference between being a business owner and not; I learned after about a decade. It's still a rat race if you do not figure out how to link up with new opportunities to serve on a regular basis.

Gone are those days when you would spend 40 hours per week on the same job for 40 years, starting at an entry-level of $40,000 annual salary. Even a 6-figure salary doesn't add up any longer.

Honestly, I am not even talking about the money because I believe that part is a by-product of having the skills to link yourself up with new opportunities to serve more consistently.

In the 9-5 world, it's about those resumes connecting with new potential employers on a consistent basis. You can no longer afford to settle with one employer for 40 years.

But in business, it's about connecting with new leads, new customers, new clients, and new deals on a consistent basis on demand. It isn't easy in a highly competitive world if you don't pay attention to digital evolution.

Think about it. How many businesses do you see on your way home with "*closing out sales?*" Every organization, including charity organizations are struggling to connect to people who can donate.

Here is the problem. The world hasn't moved on. It's moving as a consistent constant. Technology is always evolving, and I'm sorry, business cards and billboards have become the most ineffective way to connect with new opportunities to serve and of course, make more money.

So how do you connect with new leads, new prospects, new customers, new clients, new deals, new jobs, and more money as the world continues to evolve in the digital era?

You guessed it right. Digital Marketing; the art and science of leveraging digital evolution to build influence and connect your values with an audience that already wants it badly.

We called it internet marketing and online marketing just a few years ago. But the truth is that we can't keep up because there are ongoing developments around the same concept; everything is digital and digitally evolving.

In fact, sooner or later, we are going to have half-humans, half-robots taking away more old-school jobs. But the good news is that more new-school jobs are being created.

Digital marketing is a solution to the problem of connecting with new opportunities as relevant to the obsession of mankind with wanting everything easier, simpler, faster, and all the other 'er's you can think of.

But we also know that every solution creates new problems. And every problem creates new opportunities to solve more problems.

So I hope you are starting to think of the idea of digital marketing as the greatest opportunity to make more money and build out your career, your life, and your legacy, no matter what it is.

I guess the easiest proof I can offer you right now is to observe just social media, which is just one piece of many, from this lens for 24 hours. Then write your objective observations as to how much money is moving hands right in front of you in real-time.

While many businesses are going under due to what I consider as arrogance, many new companies and income opportunities are rising daily from something so obvious many still can't see it.

We are going to use this book to shed light on digital marketing and also teach the skills required to take serious advantage of it.

If you are still reading, you already know that you need to be marketing in order to keep bringing new eyeballs and revenue into your business. You already know that it's a direct source of food for the beast.

So even if you want to do great things for others from the goodness of your heart, you know that you won't be able to afford to keep it going if no revenues are coming in.

But the question now is why should you pivot from more traditional types of marketing into digital? For one, it's easier, simpler, and gets you results faster. And guess what, it's actually cheaper too.

Back in the days, a lot of marketing activity involved throwing stuff against the wall and hoping that something would stick. Quite often than none, some did stick. But I would attribute that to that particular environment where everyone else didn't know any better.

In this digital age, more and more people are discovering it, even though I believe that digital marketing is still very much in its infancy stages.

That right there is your competitive advantage going right out the window. Sure there is a balancing act between not just jumping on every bandwagon and being proactive when it comes to new technology.

Leveraging digital marketing is one of those where you have to be proactive because it has to do with the blood and life of your mission; new people to serve.

As opposed to traditional methods, everyone is equal. (I'm not sure if that's a good thing) and it's easy to get started. That could have been a disadvantage, but because getting started is readily available to anyone, most people are taking it for granted.

Many people literally had to wait years for major universities to be teaching it in their curriculum to pay attention to digital marketing. It's not too late, but that doesn't mean you didn't miss out on certain opportunities that come from taking action at ground zero.

So I get approached every now and then by people who have a little money to spend on marketing to build their movement and mission. *"Ola, I've got $25,000 to spend on marketing. Where should I start?"*

It's probably the most popular question that I get. "How do I get started?" Some would say, "there are too many people talking, exactly where is the starting point?"

That can be absolutely confusing and frustrating. So I get it. Especially when you consider the beast itself, the internet is such a viral machine that it's so easy to get lost in a rabbit hole without any chances of coming out with a useful product.

That's one of my goals with this book. I want to help you outline a step-by-step approach which obviously has to start with step one. Speaking of goals, the first step is for you to get crystal clear on what your personal and business goal is, not "are" but "is" with respect to why you want to leverage digital marketing.

Without a clearly written out goal and purpose statement, you will get lost in the sauce of the beast because what we love about it is what you may end up resenting about it.

I can't tell you how many people have left the mission because of the frustration directly linked to not starting with a goal and a clear purpose. It may sound simple, but anything worthwhile in life and business is easier said than done.

This book is a great guide, a type of bible, if you will, to help you stay grounded in your set purpose as you navigate the world of digital marketing.

That's what we are going to use as a seed for the initial research to identify the right content, platform, and placement strategy that will create your desired results from this simple process presented in this book.

Go ahead and login into your favorite social media platform right now. What do you see? I bet you see some type of news and/or post feed.

Here is something else you will notice. You will notice that the first few postings in that feed tend to be a continuation of the same type of content you had been engaging, at least with your eyes during your recent browsing.

As simple and as regular or obvious as that may sound to you right now, I want you to realize how powerful it is to follow your ideal customer and client with content they will most likely engage again.

"Again?" Yes. It's very important to pay particular attention to the idea that you can actually track the interest of your ideal audience down to what they are most likely going to enjoy and engage in. Imagine being able to track this phenomenon down to micro-behaviors and leverage it to build your ability to connect with more opportunities to serve and therefore make money.

It's been proven time and time again that your average customers will not do business with you just after their first encounter with your business. Back in the days, you would have to make follow-up calls to see if they were ready to do business.

But in the digital era, you can track and set up automated campaigns to take advantage of what we already know for centuries.

Have you experienced an ad following you to every website you go to after viewing a product you haven't yet bought? With digital marketing, you are able to track people's interest and connect it to your offer in the marketplace in an extremely predictable and scalable way.

In this digital age, you can leverage all trackable numbers to create more of its kind optimized for massive profits in your business.

Before we dive in through the rest of this book which I know you are excited about, this is what I want you to do. I want you to grab a piece of paper or open an empty document on your personal computer.

Then I want you to write straight from your heart what you want personally from digital marketing. I was hoping you could describe your desired outcome in full detail and what that desired outcome would mean to you with respect to wealth building and living a healthier lifestyle, and fostering better personal and business relationships.

Here is what's going to happen. You will discover how much you have buried inside for one. In addition to that, you will notice a flow of ideas based on what we've covered in just the introduction.

There are some exceptions. Maybe you are one of them, and you don't feel that way after honestly going through that exercise. This is what I want you to do.

I want you to describe in full detail how you've attempted to use emails and/or social media in any capacity to advance your outcome either in business or in your personal life.

Once you've done that, I want you to attempt to quantify the outcome you got from such activities in the past and then multiply it somehow by 100. Continue to describe the Product of that exercise because I know you may find it difficult at this point to describe things in discrete data.

Congratulations. You have just had your first experience in the excitement you are about to discover over the next 11 chapters of digital marketing awesomeness that's about to happen to your business and your mission.

It's never been this easy to quantify the numerous activities involved in exposing content, products, and services to quality eyeballs.   Literally, all of it and more can be done from a laptop and a decent internet connection.

In the next and first official chapter, I am going to help you a little further in defining your goals. Remember, you ultimately know what outcome you desire from leveraging digital marketing to spread your message, impact, products, and services.

But I want to help you define it so that you can predict results so you can double down over and over where necessary. No worries. It's going to be a lot of fun as we dive even further into this.

SECTION 1

THE PIECES

CHAPTER 1

The Goal

Previously in Digital Marketing Certified, I shared a little bit of my story and my path to and through digital marketing, from investing $2,000 to making $12. I also shared how it's actually worse to get stuck in a rat race as an entrepreneur.

You probably also learned for the first time that it's cheaper and much more effective and efficient to leverage digital marketing to build a business than it is to spend your hard-earned money on billboards and yellow books.

Okay. I know I didn't mention yellow books yet. But you should know that it's probably the biggest scam of the 2010s because many people still spent millions of dollars literally on those two marketing channels long after it had become obsolete. Sure we still received it at the house, but they went straight into the garbage, right?

I am glad you are still reading because we are actually just getting started. Just like the last 10 years of digital marketing, that was all introduction.

This whole thing is about to be better and more exciting. We are just scratching the surface. And I've promised from the beginning that I want to take you on a self-explanatory journey that you couldn't wait to apply it to your own businesses and endeavors.

If you are like me, you shy away from attention. It's like a taboo to seek attention beyond the average level of attention that you get when you go to work daily. But fortunately or unfortunately, you have to get attention when you have a product or service to offer. You can't get stuck with that *"I'm conservative"* excuse.

I am speaking from experience. I know it may be hard to believe but I am introverted to a large extent. My natural instinct is to keep things quiet and win quietly. But that won't work when you have a business to run with a goal to at least create a more positive impact. Precisely, you need attention.

So Lisa just wanted to make money. That was the goal she thought. She had probably spent about $2,300 or more in different digital products to make money online. Not only that, she had abandoned some other traditional businesses she was trying to build.

This was the very early days of marketing online, and it was an exciting idea, particularly for those who were tired of chasing family and friends around to support their little businesses. For some people, the goal had become to shame those who never supported them, to prove a point, or to seek validation from the wrong sources.

Lisa had just lost her life savings on investing in a traditional business, and she wanted to make some quick money so that she could prove to herself that she could do it. But that is "it?"

This is also a tell-tale sign and little-to-no wonder why she lost money in the first place. Do you notice the vague nature of her goals?

Many people jump into digital marketing, just like Lisa. It's either a goal with respect to sentiments or goals set in the wrong direction.

The truth is that there are more than enough online platforms that will take your money and send you back into the streets without apologizing. It's your responsibility to turn a profit and their responsibility to take your money in exchange for access to the advertising platform.

After my first consultation with her, it was clear to me that we couldn't move forward until I helped her set clear and concise goals. It's not as easy as it sounds.

"What's your goal?" "I want to get more clients." "Why?" "Because I want to." "Okay. I can't help you." "Why not?" "Because I can't." "Okay thanks." That's literally but probably an oversimplified version of the conversations.

But it's actually worse now because anyone can jump on an advertising platform and lose money because it's accessible.

Many online and social media ad platforms are advertising the easy-to-get-started message. So people are jumping on, setting up an account without setting goals properly.

Digital marketing is a beautiful development in recent and modern times, but there are more variables and layers to it than a typical human mind can contain or sustain at any point in time.

Therefore it's easy to lose track of activities and potentially lose money just by the mere fact that you **know what you want.** You know your business more than anyone else and I'm sure you think you know who your ideal customers and clients are.

But that's a problem. Let me explain.

There is always a blindspot for everything you know about anything in life. You can also think of such blindspots as a function of your biases based on your past experiences. Traditionally, that would be good enough to carry you for up to 5 years or even more with advertising your Product and services.

However, like everything else now in the human experience, what you knew yesterday can be easily obsolete today just like that. Things are moving so fast that the human brain can't keep up. And what does this have to do with setting goals in digital marketing?

Wait. I'll get there. As I was saying, you think you know your business. In fact, you too have your social media profile and participate as a consumer on those various platforms; but that's it. As a consumer, you know these things.

This book focuses on what it takes to be a profitable producer for various digital platforms. Everything happens so fast, and it will be a losing battle to attempt to keep up with it just by knowing what you want.

Knowing what you want is not enough to run digital marketing campaigns successfully. It's precisely a good way to lose money or lose time and energy or run campaigns that will frustrate you and make you resent the idea of digital marketing altogether.

Instead, I want to help you set smart goals. S.M.A.R.T goals. I promise. I am not talking about vision boards. And I am not knocking vision boards either. But they can be as vague as they get.

Knowing what you want is a good place to start, but it needs to be aligned with quantifiable business goals and objectives.

Too many people work for 10 years or more, save good money and build excellent credit, run to the bank to get a loan... Just off knowing what they want.

I have way too many stories of people who have had to start from scratch like that. Some of them even lose their family because of the financial stress on the relationships they care about. I can tell you that it starts from the foundation.

Once you've identified what you want from digital marketing, be it leads, sales, customers, clients, deals, or to recruit quality team members into your organization, then it's time to put that into black and white, assess and align with your business goals.

I want you to trace it to actual profits or whatever you want to call it in order to be able to afford to do it. The way I was raised, I also tend to shy away from the idea of maximizing profits. So I understand when people say things like, *"I just want to help people."*

That's cute. But you also want to be able to afford to do it over and over again. Breaking even on the money, time, and energy you spend on either a for-profit or non-profit organization will end up frustrating the whole thing. And then it becomes pointless.

So it's very important to align what you want out of this with maximizing profits and business goals in order to define goals and business objectives properly for your digital marketing efforts. It is destructive behavior to suggest anything less than spelling it out like this for you.

Your goals need to be defined in a quantifiable manner. Remember, this was all about finding new opportunities to serve.

This could be a new student for your school or course, a new customer for your business, a new client for your private consulting practice, a new deal, etc.

The bottom line is that these are people that will go from awareness of what you have to offer to consideration of your Product or service and then hopefully to conversion. You could be a pastor, and we could be talking about attracting new members to your church.

So this is going to be an experience for them from awareness or discovery to conversion. What are your goals? And how soon do you want to accomplish the goals?

In addition to that, I want you to be aware that the experience of your ideal customer, client, or member will happen in segments. Some of them will discover you and convert to a customer right away, and some will not convert till two years later and everything in between. Oh… and some will never convert.

You will set high-level goals, and you will also set goals to optimize the experience of the audience firstly by building brand and influence. *"Branding and influence"* all in itself sound vague, but we are able to quantify and track progress with digital marketing.

Back in 2009, when I first stumbled into digital marketing, it was easy to set up an experience and make money without branding, but competition is a bit higher right now as digital marketing becomes more popular.

How do we know? We set high-level goals such as a specific amount like, say… One Million Dollars in Sales in

One Year, but we also set micro-goals at every segment in your customer's experience.

A smart goal will also help in a feasibility study before wasting your hard-earned money on a project that will lead nowhere. Digital Marketing is for everyone but every campaign type is not for every business type. A smart goal will help us further in a feasibility study of a good campaign fit among so many opportunities.

Let's spell out smart goals. S.M.A.R.T. And let's break it down. I did not create this. From a little research, I found out that the smart goal is a concept that was created in 1981 by George T. Doran. Since I've personally learned about it, I've also seen different versions of it.

S for <u>Specific</u> - Your goal needs to be one thing at least defined as that… at a high level first before we break it down using a process called CBS (Campaign Breakdown Structure).

There is a book I will recommend and link up in the reference section at the end of this book called "ONE THING" by Gary Keller to help you understand the concept even more.

M for <u>Measurable</u> - The project management institute (PMI) called this "meaningful." I think that is interesting.

What it means (no pun intended) is that you can actually measure your goal and therefore be able to track progress toward achieving it. "Speaking of achieving it…"

A for <u>Achievable</u> - How realistic is this goal? I know you may have heard and believe in all types of manifestations of your desires and all types of Jedi mind tricks and techniques to attract what you want in life, and I believe in those things too.

But when you are setting up digital marketing campaigns that involve spending time, energy, and possibly your hard-earned money, I want you to ensure that you are doing so with respect to a realistically achievable goal.

The manifestation stuff depends on hope as a strategy, but successful digital marketing campaigns depend on setting specific, meaningful, and achievable goals.

Do you have the skills to achieve the goals? If you don't, does someone on your team have the skills? Or do you have access to the necessary education to acquire the skills? That is obviously a *"yes"* because this is a great start in that direction.

If you will be dropping this book before you complete it, it's best to throw any digital marketing-related goals in the trash already, and it will save you so much headache.

Without direct or indirect access to the required skills and resources, especially education, you will lose money in digital marketing, and it's worse if you lose it in the form of time and energy.

You can make money back but you can't get time back. When people waste time, they usually do not value and track their time properly.

R for <u>Relevant</u> - I've seen other versions labeling this as realistic. But that would probably correlate more with the previous one, which is "achievable."

The relevance factor is another level of ensuring your goal for a digital marketing campaign aligns with your overall business objective. If it doesn't, it becomes another distraction.

Personally, I resent all forms of distractions in business because, frankly, I've been a victim of distractions multiple times in my business career.

Also, some of the advertising (or ad) platforms on which you will be setting campaigns have metrics for measuring relevance factors and quality scores, even at micro levels. So I want you to start adopting that mindset right now already at this higher level.

T for Time-Bound - And again, PMI called this *"timely."* Remember, we are not just setting a goal of one million dollars in that previous example, and we are setting a time frame because of the dangers of Parkinson's law.

What is Parkinson's Law?

Parkinson's Law is the old adage that work expands to fill the time allotted for its completion. The term was first coined by Cyril Northcote Parkinson in an essay he wrote for "The Economist" in 1955.

When you don't set the desired achievement time on a goal, you are still setting a time, forever or never. These are terrible timeframes for business. In fact, the ad platforms will stop taking your money eventually because they are set up to only work for folks who know what they are doing.

The whole point of this is to reiterate and reemphasize the importance of defining success upfront and subsequently avoiding unnecessary disappointments with your digital marketing campaigns. It's a mindset, and it's the proper foundation before engaging too far and in too deep.

Here is an example of a goal statement.

Specific - *"I want to write a book called Digital Marketing Certified (DMC)."*

Measurable - *"The book will have a minimum of 10 chapters and 30,000 words between 150 and 200 pages."*

Achievable - *"Because I am busy with other endeavors, I can realistically achieve writing this book in about 12 weeks."*

Relevant - *"Digital Marketing Certified (DMC) is relevant to my overall business goals because it will educate my friends on what I do, help me get more students and clients, educate my future clients first, and more importantly* make projects 1,000 times easier for the team and stakeholders."

Time-Bound - *"The book will be ready for publishing in 12 weeks because I am committed to releasing a video version weekly on my YouTube channel (www.YouTube.com/OLATuxAbitogun) until release."*

I know what you are thinking. *"OLA, what about an actual digital marketing goal statement example?"*

I got you.

Specific - *"I want to generate new clients at the $7,500 price point into my consulting business with digital marketing."*

Measurable - *"I want to generate 13 new clients into my consulting business."*

Achievable - *"I have 2 clients already generated from my traditional last word-of-mouth campaign leveraging a messaging app broadcast.*

I have generated some revenue, streamlined by prospecting process, and I can do this 13 more times definitely."

Relevant - *"Getting 13 month more clients will not just put me at 15 clients which aligns with my overall business goals, it will also bring in more revenue so that I can invest in more efficient processes, acquire more resources and build my team. I don't want to be a slave to the business."*

Time-Bound - *"I want to acquire all 13 new clients in the next 90 days."*

So this is what I want you to do. Open an empty document on Google Docs and write your very own goal statement. If I were you and I am completely new to digital marketing, I would definitely print it out for my desk.

In the next chapter, we will dive into the next piece of the pieces that you need to understand deeply in order to create successful and profitable digital marketing campaigns.

Like me, I know you want to serve many people. But you must understand these people as individuals first and not as a group in order to create the most optimized impact as aligned with your overall business goals.

CHAPTER 2

The Person(s)

Exactly who are you trying to serve by leveraging digital marketing? I know you want to make more money. But where is this money coming from?

Money comes from only one place. It doesn't fall from the sky, and we do not pluck it from a tree. It comes from other people. The money you are going to make comes from other people, right?

In the previous chapter, we talked about setting goals, smart goals, to be precise. We also talked about why the desire to help someone is not enough to run a successful digital marketing campaign.

It definitely is not enough to "want" to be an entrepreneur. I also want to be Elon Musk within the next 24 hours. It's highly unlikely that's going to happen, right?

So the act of "wanting something" is not enough. You will increase your chances of success when you set specific, meaningful, measurable, and achievable goals.

We also discussed the differences between setting goals at micro and macro levels of the experience for your prospects, customers, clients, partners, and your audience.

And I gave you actionable steps and real-life examples of goal statements. That exercise was necessary because it represents the foundation of your journey in your digital marketing endeavors.

You will encounter multiple layers of variables that can turn into very complex problems that can potentially include losing serious money and, worse, time and energy.

So it's important always to reference that chapter if you ever feel lost in your business with regard to marketing and promotion in a digital age.

As a typical human being, you will get in over your head and lose focus at some point. It's inevitable. But you can always trace your step backward as far as to your original smart goal when necessary. I promise. It will happen.

In this chapter, we will talk about the person, not the people. I know I just said money comes from people. But if you don't understand these people at a person-by-person level, you will miss it completely. Hence this lesson is presented as a full-blown chapter.

In December 2004, during my first encounter with real estate, I was so excited that I dropped a private class I was taking in mobile application development. Those were the days when you couldn't watch long videos in the palm of your hands on the go.

We were learning coding, programming, and simulating everything you know today as your smartphone in virtual environments. It was also my senior year studying Computer Engineering at the New Jersey Institute of Technology (NJIT).

A friend of mine (his real name starts with an 'F,' but I will call him Jason)... He had informed me about a real estate home-buying seminar in East Orange, New Jersey, which he never showed up to. But I was sucked into real estate for life. It hit home for me.

Wow. I could just leverage mortgages to become a landlord who collects money month in and month out. So I started going on appointments to look at every house listed on the market, starting with one house in Belleville... even though my credit score would have put me in a terrible position of the high-interest rate at the time.

The mortgage officer at the seminar had told me that my "500 and change" credit score would get me a property, and I would become a landlord in a few weeks. A few weeks later, I stumbled into a late-night infomercial, and before I knew it, I ended up at another seminar that cost $3,000 that I didn't have.

My friend Jason had agreed to partner up with me leveraging his credit card in exchange for paying it back in a few weeks with interest. Again, Jason did not show up, but I was so excited that I could never forget that generosity as a foundation for what I am sharing with you today.

If he had shown up, I would have ended up on the wrong path, which involved just any house without proper assessment. But what do I mean by assessment?

You see... Jason had agreed to partner up to buy a bunch of houses with me but not having easy access to buying by myself led me down the route of learning marketing properly. At first, it was about real estate, right?

What I eventually learned is that it wasn't about houses and real estate per se. It was more so about finding deals and creating a profitable path starting from the beginning.

And that wasn't the end of it. Profitable deals are sourced from real people's stories and real-life problems.

The common denominator in all of that and across multiple types of businesses is people, the endless questions they have in life, and the inevitable problems they face in the pursuit of happiness. And in order to understand your market at a basic and foundational level, it's wiser to understand "the person."

So in the rest of this book, we may call it your market, audience, people, avatars, or people. Who is the ideal person that your product, service, or offer is designed for?

This person has a problem, a question, or a void, and your business's value is designed to fill that void.

The biggest mistake that the losers of digital marketing are making today is the assumption that everyone is their ideal customer. As soon as you post something on social media, you are asked to boost it with $10 in ad spend. And after spending that $10, it's crickets.

Of course, anyone can become a connection to an ideal client for your business, but it's not wise to throw time, energy, and money at everyone's attention without proper market research and analysis. You will lose money.

There are two parts to market research and analysis, which are necessary if you spend your hard-earned resources on digital marketing. The first part is about determining the market size. The second part is to realistically figure out how much of that market share you can cover; competition analysis.

It's very likely that you are not the first to offer the solution that your product and services offer, right? And if you are the first, that is not necessarily a smart move; you better know what you are doing.

Many times, I hear aspiring entrepreneurs proudly boast about being the first to do something. Listen. It's most likely that you will not be Bill Gates or Elon Musk. These are historical "firsts" of tools that we all enjoy today, but this kind of entrepreneur comes but once in a lifetime.

So let's be realistic. Your product, service, offer, and/or business has direct and indirect competition, which means you will not be able to capture 100% of the market share.

The market is going to have segments that are highly competitive and other segments with low competition. The low-competition segments also tend to have a lower market share percentage.

But the real question is this. Is there a market? Is there a "person" who has a direct or indirect need for the solution that your business offers? If there are, how many persons can we realistically identify?

Last but not least, is there any other business or anyone else already providing a similar or indirect solution to these people's problems?

These questions must be answered before you try to set up a digital marketing campaign to avoid losing money or, worse, time and energy.

Let's make it clear.

1. Market Size
2. Competition Analysis

When you determine the size of the market first, you are able to decide from the beginning if a market or business is worth going after or not. If you don't, you may just be moving off your own passion-driven biases. As a human being, you naturally gravitate toward certain types of businesses for different reasons.

Maybe a friend of yours seems to be enjoying a business model, and the reality is that you truly do not know the intricacies of what it takes to be in that business successfully or to look like success on the outside.

You don't know what you do not know. Many businesses are laundromats, and many people will take Peter's money to pay Paul just to look like success on the outside.   And many do that as a strategy of hope, and hope is a terrible marketing and business strategy.

So instead of operating your marketing from a place of hope down the line, you are able to assess the market size and see upfront if it's worth going into a particular business or not.

The same is applicable at the micro level of a business. You may be considering opening a different department. It's going to cost you time, energy, money, and other types of resources. Before engaging those resources, determine the market size and do a competition analysis.

You may identify some risk, and you may just identify an opportunity bigger than what you envisaged. The benefits of doing this assessment are much more than avoiding a negative risk. It's just a profitable habit to get into overall as an existing or aspiring entrepreneur.

There are simple, fun, free, and paid tools to perform market research and competition analysis. But they are useless if you don't even know what you are looking for. The most popular of them is the almighty search engine; Google.

At press time, Google is the biggest and most popular search engine that we all run to when we have a question. Dare I say, almost all research starts from Google, including medical research by a medical doctor who may be getting ready to put an incision in you or your children's body.

I know that's scary, right? But that's the reality. I don't know when you are reading this book, and I don't know tomorrow. Hopefully, I will continue to get the opportunity to update and offer new versions as we evolve into an ever-evolving digital world.

So maybe the hottest search engine when you are reading this won't be Google, but it will always be some kind of search Engine. As humans, we are always searching, asking, and creating new problems to solve. If you understand this, you will always be in business successfully.

Whatever your biggest and most popular search engine is will be your number one market research and analysis tool. Not the only one but always a great place to start from.

You can start by searching a seed keyword or keyword phrase on the search engine. What you will discover is the beginning of a journey through a rabbit hole with lots of useful information that will fuel your present level of excitement about the business you are trying to initiate.

This information will be grouped into a group of seven different categories listed as follows or similar.

Category Number 1: Observe the top 10 results generated by the search engine result page, also known as the SERPS. Open each one of the results and see how your competitors are already offering solutions to your market. Also, determine how many pages are offering results already.

Category Number 2: Observe the top 10 automatically suggested searches by the search box. As you are typing your seed keyword or keyword phrase, you may notice that the search area is also auto-suggesting and attempting to populate the area ahead of you.

Take note of the different phrases from the artificial intelligence of the search engine. Each one of these is likely an additional opportunity for you to serve and make more money.

Category Number 3: Observe the *"People also ask"* section of the SERP. You will see the question that other people similar to people who search your seed keyword or keyword phrase are searching on the search engine. These are additional opportunities that most people engaging in digital marketing are not taking advantage of.

Category Number 4: If you are trying this on a smart mobile phone, I want you to observe the *"People also search for"* section for more ideas on angles to serve this market from.

Quick question. How many people advertising online today would you guess are patient enough to do this much market research before wasting thousands of dollars on digital marketing?

Category Number 5: There is another section that may not show on every device called the "Refine This Search" section. You should pay attention to it. This machine attempts to help your audience narrow their search faster and easier to the answer.

The machines don't create these answers from thin air. These are answers from your competitors being fed to a person who is potentially an ideal client of yours. When they are ready to spend money, guess whose pocket that money is going into. Your guess is as good as mine.

Category Number 6: Sometimes, your seed keyword or keyword phrase is too narrow for the search engines to find meaningful results, and it can tell because of the growing machine learning and artificial intelligence technology.

So there is a section mostly on smart mobile phones called *"Broaden This Search"* on the SERP. This section will give additional ideas of exactly what is in the mind of that person that potentially and possibly desperately needs your service.

Category Number 7: This section is probably the one you are familiar with if you also use Google to answer every question that comes to mind like me. It's called the "Related Searches" section, and it's usually at the bottom of the screen if you are on a desktop.

If this section is populated, it's an indicator that there is a market for the business you have in mind.

This is what I want you to do. I want you to come up with a seed keyword phrase for your business using this formula. The phrase will start with one of seven different types of phrases.

1. "I want to…"
2. "How to…"
3. "How do I"
4. "How can I…"
5. "What is…"
6. "Where is the nearest…"
7. "Where is the closest…"

I want you to end each one of those phrases with a phrase that represents what your business offers.

For example, my digital marketing consulting business market research would start with *"I want to market my business on Google."* Another example could be *"where is the nearest digital marketing consultant?"*

Come up with 100 different phrases like that for your business and attempt to search each one of them on your favorite search engine like Google, Yahoo, or YouTube, which is the 2nd biggest search engine at press time.

The top of the search engine result page will actually tell you how many results are generated. That's a starting indicator of how many pages are competing for the attention of your ideal person, audience, market, customer, or client.

After this exercise, you would have gotten to know that "person" a little more. And that means you are better equipped to serve the person a little bit more than your average competitor. It's a competitive advantage at worst.

Most people will shy away from this exercise, which increases your chances of dominating your market and leaving scraps for the rest.

These persons that your business will serve are in two different categories. They are probably searching for a solution already, and secondly, they are already following your competitor.

Market research and competition analysis gives you an opportunity to find out where they are spending their time with that smart device in their hands and legally stealing them from your competitors.

The first category is called the intent-based market audience, and the second category is called the interrupt market audience. Let's quickly break it down.

The **intent-based market audience** is actively in the middle of intentionally searching and looking for a solution that your business provides.

On the flip side, the **interrupt-based market audience** is not actively searching for a solution, but we've been able to track their activities online and determine their interest based on their online behavior.

In that case, they would be interrupted in the middle of other unrelated activities online in order to get into their discovery zone. The journey of your ideal "person(s)" travels through four main stages, namely:

1. Discovery
2. Awareness
3. Consideration and…
4. Conversion

In chapter 3, we will be diving through "value," how to identify it, and leverage it to create a smooth transition for your person(s) and the market, from discovery all the way through conversion into a customer and long-term client and even beyond.

In fact, with this same concept, you will be able to turn a decent percentage of your best clients into loyal evangelists for your business, therefore, creating even more revenue, all thanks to value.

CHAPTER 3

The Value

It means a lot of different things to people depending on where they are standing. But in this chapter, my goal is first to make sure we are standing in the same position before extracting the actual value I want to share with you.

You are reading this book because you are trying to build a business or organization of some sort, right? If that's the case, keep reading.

In the last chapter, we talked about "the person(s)" as one of the pillars we must clearly identify before trying to set up marketing campaigns in the digital era. A failure to do this will simply defeat the purpose, which I am hoping is partly the benefit of tracking down every penny and making sure it doubles itself.

You also learned how my 500 and change in credit score saved me from early life bankruptcy. Personally, I've had some ups and downs naturally in the type of risky and non-conventional journey I chose to embark on; becoming an entrepreneur. But it's never gotten so bad that I had to file for bankruptcy. Thank goodness.

More importantly, you also learned how a lack of proper market research and competition analysis could result in losing your life savings and/or capital, $10 at a time. We reviewed the dangers of passion-driven biases, the greatest market research tool, which is free, seed keyword and keyword phrases, the role of Artificial Intelligence and Machine Learning in market research and more.

Last and definitely not all, and for sure not least, we talked about the two different categories of your ideal customer and client and the four stages they have to travel in order to not just maximize profits for your business but to deliver value.

And speaking of value, I became dangerous and over-valued for the 9-5 world since I learned what you are about to discover in this chapter.

It was 2014, and I had been helping quite a few people I met in the internet and network marketing world make their first $100, $1,000, $200,000, and even $4 million completely online. Not just that, I did very well with my business too.

But the honest truth is that I had not fully grasped the magnitude of the value in what I had learned. On my best day ever, I was able to use written text and words to convert complete strangers into $15,000 in sales. And I did it multiple times over. Somehow, I had acquired a skill set that could collect such an amount of money in exchange for a digital product without being physically present to sell.

Before that, my best day ever was back in real estate when I closed a deal that created a net profit of $82,000.

But let's put things into perspective, right? There are a lot of things that go into the process of closing real estate deals, and it wasn't easy, to say the least. I could potentially sit around for months and not close another deal.

In addition to that, a whole real estate property belonging to a person or a family is involved. It's a big deal in terms of vested interest involved when a decision is made to buy or sell real estate in comparison to an online transaction, especially back then.

But these days, people are more comfortable with purchasing a whole car online. So it's actually gotten a whole lot easier, provided you are able to communicate the value proposition effectively.

I will forever be grateful to gentlemen Mike Dillard and Ben Settle for learning these skill sets from them as far back as 2009/2010. I do not think they know who I am at all. But it doesn't matter because you are about to learn the skills more than 10 years later.

Sales is hard for an average human being. Most people are only comfortable selling a resume. And to be honest, it's because of the dependency on the credentials and the experience to do the selling for them in a non-confrontational way.

It's actually similar to why an estimated 77% of people hate public speaking. According to many studies, people actually fear public speaking more than death. They get bombarded by panic and a paralyzing fear of guess what, rejection. I personally still hate the feeling of being rejected.

When you pay close attention to what I just said, it's not the actual rejection. It's the "feeling" of being rejected that paralyzes people to avoid sales, public speaking, or being in any position where the ultimate desire is to be accepted. It's fascinating to know.

So many people fantasize about the idea of a big business. But then the fear of being rejected becomes a huge huddle in their way, directly or indirectly.

Even if you are a person who is naturally okay with sales, it's a challenge to build a sales team with a decent attrition rate which is the rate at which people leave your organization or team. People find it a lot easier to use a resume or CV to sell their time in exchange for less than $50 per hour than to sell even air to breathe.

You can invent the best product in the world. If you are terrible at communicating the value of it to a prospect, you won't be able to afford its production sooner or later.

Another struggle is the inability of a lot of people to know the difference between personal values and the value of a product for prospects.

Why do people window-shop? I'll tell you why. A prospect can want a product and not be able to afford it.

Sometimes, it's just the wrong timing. But that's not the reason why people are not buying your product or services.

People choose not to purchase from you because you failed to transfer enough value in a way that is valuable to them. It was a negative choice against added value for your business.

Value in this context is in the eyes of the user or consumer and not in the eyes of the producer. Value is absolutely not an objective truth; it's subjective, but only until you learn what I want to share with you right now.

So it's one thing to know the benefit of your product or service; it's completely another thing to know how to transfer the value of those benefits to the prospects in order to buy now.

I am sure you have probably learned about the differences between features and benefits before. Well, this is an additional layer to the madness. But when you master this skill set, you will become dangerously profitable as your competitors drown in debt.

Oxford dictionary calls sales the exchange of a commodity for money, but it also calls it the action of selling something. But then what is selling? If you are able to transfer value to your potential customers and clients at scale using written words, what would that mean for your business?

According to INC magazine, a Harvard professor says 95% of purchasing decisions are subconscious. I personally learned a long time ago that 85% of sales are initiated emotionally, and they justify with logic later.

So while you may present with all the facts and figures to back up your own version of the value that the product and services offer, you will fail 85%-95% of the time because you are selling the wrong value to the wrong side of the human mind. It's a hard pill to swallow.

Have you ever heard the saying, "Facts tell, but story sells?" Storytelling is a highly profitable skill to learn, and no amount of facts, data and statistics can engage the human mind like a good story. It's not necessarily the easiest thing to do, but it's non-negotiable when we create an offer.

The key to successfully transferring the value to your prospect, or dare I say, sometimes manufacturing value out of thin air in a way that is perceived by your prospect, is to tap into their real motivation to buy. I promise you. It has nothing to do with doing the "right" thing.

Why do people buy? Seriously, why do people buy into anything, ideas, ideologies, belief system, a product, a service, or anything? What motivates them to buy? By now, you should get the gist. It's not logical.

Is it because they need it, they want it, or can afford it? Let's be honest. People buy things they can't afford all the time, right?

In fact, for every time you engage unnecessary empathy around the decision of a person not buying from you for affordability reasons, they probably just spent ten times your price on a ten times worse competitor's product or service. So affordability is rarely even a motivator to buy a product or not.

There are many motivation theories from numerous studies, and I love them all. But allow me to share a few with you, and then I will share my favorite.

Maslow's need hierarchy theory is based on people's five basic needs; survival, safety, love or belonging, self-esteem and self-actualization. I personally would add "a sense of" to each one of those because people don't even assess those things logically, and they are mostly based on feelings at an emotional level.

Also, there is the Herzberg's motivational and hygiene factors. Have you heard of McClelland's human motivation theory which states that every person has one of three main driving motivators: the need for achievement, affiliation (sounds like belonging again), or power? These are all mindsets.

People would buy things just because of a sense of belonging, even when it directly offers no tangible value to them. So when designing a marketing and sales message around your product and service, you have to be careful with your definition of value.

The key thing to always remember is that it's in the eyes of your prospect and rarely ever about your personal belief system. While you should be absolutely confident about the value you feel your product and service offers, you need to remain aware that it's about making that confidence contagious enough for the prospect to feel that level of confidence, pull the credit card out, and buy now.

So you have managed to come up with a good product in your opinion. People are checking it out, but they are not buying. In fact, you know a few of these prospects personally, and you've deemed their excuses legitimate enough to keep looking for the right customer.

NEWSFLASH: It's either you haven't made an offer, or you've got a bad offer. What is an offer, and how is that different from a product?

An offer is a presentation of a product beyond just the product. Some kind of tangible or intangible element has been added to make the product compelling enough to make them buy now. In essence, a product is just a product but "buy and get one free" is an offer.

The product will always be available, but there is no guarantee that the offer will be available if you do not buy it right now. As for intangibles, the same can be said about "a limited time" discounted price. Again, the product or at least an indirect competition to the product will always be available, but there is no guarantee there will be a discount at a later time.

But these are the obvious ones you've encountered at a mall before. Let's get back to using text and words to make a prospect buy from you now and not later. It's nothing other than your ability to communicate the value proposition with the subconscious mind.

My favorite of the motivation theories is said to have been birthed by Sigmund Freud, but it was made famous by Abraham Maslow. I discovered it through Tony Robbins.

The six basic human needs are love or connection, variety, significance, certainty, growth, and contribution. If you are able to stimulate a sense of these needs at a subconscious and emotional level inside of your prospect's mind, you will damn near print money on demand.

It looks like spelling and tracing out an emotional journey from discovery to feeling absolutely stupid for not figuring out a way to buy now. Sure there will be situations where a buyer is unable to buy. But what you want is for your prospects to send messages expressing their fear of missing out on an offer.

If you can craft a message in a way that they feel left out if they don't buy, the idea of buying is exciting, they can feel a sense of certainty in the promised transformation into the desired state of some kind of advancement, they feel even more important, and feel like your offer will make them create the desired impact on society, then your product will have a chance of delivering the value it was intended for.

A good product or service solves a problem, answers a question, or replaces pain with pleasure or relief. Stating out the features, benefits, problem, solution, question and answer is not enough.

You will create more customers and clients in your business when you spell out the pain, the desired pleasure, or relief, especially when you are able to qualify them from a place of feelings or emotions.

Can you use words to communicate the expected transformation? Can you imagine what the pain of the present state of your customer feels like? When you can communicate the emotional state after your product and service's transformation, you will dominate your market.

As I told you towards the end of the last chapter, your customer will travel through four main stages namely:

1. Discovery
2. Awareness
3. Consideration and…
4. Conversion

The transition between each one of these stages is a conversion, and you are responsible for persuading your prospect through each one of these transitions and segments. In digital marketing, we use a mix of words, images, videos, and creatives to compel them to advance to the next level or segment.

This is what I want you to do in order to put a seal on the secret you just discovered in this chapter. There are some copy elements I want you to start paying attention to in the various marketing messages that you encounter henceforth, and I promise. You will start noticing them on all your favorite social media platforms now. You probably found this book through one of my ad creatives and copy.

For the rest of this book, we may refer to the front-end discovery-level marketing message as creatives. It simply means the actual visuals that you see first, be it words, images, videos, slides, etc. The idea is to get you to a space where you are absolutely intentional about how you craft the message.

Most of the social media platforms land you on a news feed as soon as you log in. That space is one of the most valuable spaces on the whole internet, and the platforms are very aware of that. That's why they sell opportunities to post your messages on the news feed for a fee.

It's the same concept of the newspaper selling ad spaces inside a newspaper and other news channels since ancient Roman times. When you manage to get your message on these pages, you have three seconds or less to capture the attention of your ideal audience and sell them on advancing from discovery to awareness.

It's in your best interest to learn the art and sciences of using words and text to persuade your audience to take the actions you desire on your creatives. It's called copywriting, and the elements in it are called 'copy".

You can also use the same skill set in presentation to capture the heart of a c-suite panelist and get them to buy your offers. In fact, this understanding will be responsible for your ability to create irresistible offers.

When your prospect resists your offers, they will lose sleep over it and will not have peace until they come back and buy your product and services. It has nothing to do with the actual product. But it has everything to do with how owning your product or using your service makes them feel.

When you see a post with the label **"Sponsored"** next to it, become obsessed with the "copy ."Can you see how the copywriter was able to capture your attention? What color combinations are used? What solution is being offered to solve what problem and how do they promise some kind of relief to what pain?

Go ahead, save as many sponsored feed posts as possible, and review and study them as if your life depended on it. They will become a swipe file of creatives to model your execution after when we get to that stage.

In the next section, we will start talking about the processes and how you can automate more than 90% of it to get more leads, customers, clients, and more deals. We are going to start with the process that connects the persons, as discussed in chapter 2 with the value as we have just discussed in this chapter.

SECTION 2

THE PROCESSES

CHAPTER 4

The Connection

So there are two types of connections I would like to share with you. The first type of connection is how you digitally connect the value we identified in chapter 3 with the person(s) we identified in chapter 2. And the second type of connection we will discuss is how to connect your brand with the person(s) mentally.

Let's take it backwards a little bit. In the previous chapter, we talked about value.   You learned how 85-90% of actions and acquisitions are initiated and triggered as emotional reactions; some justify with logic later.

We also reviewed a little about the motivation theories and how your competitors are probably selling products that have only 10% of the value you offer at 10 times of your prices. And they are selling them almost effortlessly to people that may not be able to afford it ordinarily.

We reminded ourselves of the six basic human needs, certainty, variety, significance, contribution, growth, and connection. And we discussed how you could use it almost to seem like you are creating value out of thin air.

When your message or "the value" covers just three of these six needs, it will simply come off as stupid for your person(s) to pass on your offer.

Every website, webpage, video, image, and blog post on your hubs needs to be exchanging value with the users. A part of the value is the user experience. How they feel as they travel that journey from discovery to conversion is your responsibility precisely because it's ultimately valuable to you and the business you are building.

What you are offering may be the best in the market, but we may never find out if whatever that is doesn't translate to what is valuable to your users. It's not just the product; it's everything, even at the most micro-levels, that they will encounter in the process of interacting with your business; the experience.

So we now have to expand a little bit on value creation to create and establish strong connections digitally and mentally with your person(s). How do you show up in their dreams at night and stress the sh*t out of their sleep if they don't buy?

1995-1996… Owo. Ondo State, Nigeria, West Africa. I was a 15 or 16 years old teenager. I would go visit my father in the office during the day where he was serving as a General Manager at his Uncle's company.

I had been going to the office for a few years during holidays, but I did it more after graduating high school. I didn't go to University right away because we had opted for me to come back to the United States after 12 of my developing years in Nigeria.

I was at home for two years, filling the gap of time, just waiting to secure accommodation in the States. My father had wanted me to study Architecture; that was his dream.

But one day, during another visit to his office, I found out that becoming an architect wasn't my dream. It was the first time a website was opened in front of me on a 3 piece-suite equipment; a personal computer. The secretary at the office was testing it out, and he would try numerous times to connect to the internet.

Thinking about it now, it was a painful process... But not really, because the frame of reference did not involve a broadband connection as we know it today.

It was exciting that he literally pulled up Toyota's website that never could load a full Toyota logo; the connection was too slow. There was a blue placeholder, but it was fascinating enough at the time. I've never left computing since then.

During that short break between high school and returning to continue schooling and life in the States, I went to the next biggest city, Akure, where I spent three months and became certified in Database Management.

I shared this story with you to establish a connection between you and the fact that the internet has grown from about 40 million users in 1995 to more than 5 billion users at press time. If internet users are increasing at that pace, producers are consistently connecting them to value increasingly and making a stupid amount of money doing it.

Most websites back in 1995 were designed to provide information and not initiate transactions. But it's a different story today. You can now buy a whole car on the internet and have it delivered to your home.

Therefore it's no longer enough to show a logo and the company's mission statement. Many businesses still have websites that can't exchange money for products and services. A lot of them felt the heat and disadvantages of that in 2020 when covid hit our world.

My business doubled in that particular year because I was positioned to serve that market right from home. Sadly, many established businesses went under for not paying attention in all these years.

You have created the right offer. And you have done the market research and identified the right audience, the gurus, and the brands they are presently following.

In fact, you are already paying time and money to attract them as visitors to your website. But the traffic is not converting to sales quickly enough for you. And you figured it's probably because you are just not getting enough traffic to the website.

So you have to come up with more funds to buy marketing and advertising in the hopes that enough prospects will convert to customers. Soon enough, you discover that you are just multiplying your problems with money you don't have and garnering more debt.

It's not working. You quit and ran back to giving away free money to the agencies that still want to sell you newspaper and yellow book ads. Do yellow books still exist?

It is important to pre-design and pre-determine how you want to connect your value (the offer) to the person(s) based on what type of pre-framing the person(s) (the prospect) had been exposed to.

When your prospects know, like and trust you, they will buy without too much effort from you. Forget about that; when they *feel* like they know, like and trust you, they will buy even more from you. All of that is emotionally and mentally triggered if you know what you are doing.

I call it the KLT factor. Does the prospect feel like they know, like and trust you? If you can't answer that question, you are probably going to struggle with converting prospects to customers, clients, and deals.

We use a formula called the **"ILSDTRR"** to build your KLT factor (a.k.a brand equity) in the digital space. The acronym stands for invest, learn, share, do, teach, refine and repeat. Let's break it down.

The idea is to build digital agents and leave thousands of your footprints everywhere in the digital space without burning your resources up while doing it. If you follow me on social media, you can see us practicing what we preach with literally thousands of videos and articles everywhere.

This is it. I want you to INVEST time and possibly money in LEARNING, then SHARING what you are learning as often as possible via online videos, blog posts, infographics, and more. After that, you actually want to DO (execute on) what you are learning in order to create experience or tacit knowledge.

If your business module permits it, you can build your business even faster by taking the sharing to the next level, which is actually TEACHING from your knowledge and experience for a fee or more KLT factor and brand equity.

Then I want you to refine and repeat that process over and over again in order to create a massive web of nodes that link back to your hub. When you do this, you will build a massive brand equity that makes it super simple to connect your value to your person(s).

All these digital agents that you are creating will work for you forever. You can't erase them off the internet if you try to after a while. And that is a good thing.

This is what I meant earlier when I mentioned pre-framing the prospects ahead of actually presenting them with an offer. The connection doesn't start at the sales presentation, and it starts before they even discover there is something to buy from you.

How cool would it be if your prospects are already asking you where to sign up before knowing if you have anything to sell or not? That's the outcome of orchestrating a strong connection of value with your audience upfront.

By positioning yourself and your brand to help your audience by actually helping them, their minds are pre-framed to recognize your brand and business as their problem solver.

Sure, a properly scripted sales presentation is still necessary because some of them may have skipped to that part in your customer journey. But most of your time, energy, and resource is best spent steering new prospects through a discovery point where you are actually helping them first before asking them to pay for something.

They usually start off with a question to answer or a problem to solve. Most people appreciate some useful information first before attempting to sell them on buying stuff.

In fact, there is a sector of your market where price point is not a determining factor in their buying decision-making process.

It boils down to the KLT factor and brand equity. They need to feel like they know, like and trust you. And then, they will pull out a credit card if anything remotely looks like their problem is solved.

The return on investment in learning, sharing, doing, teaching, refining, and repeating is literally infinite, especially if you add consistency to it.

In the world of digital marketing, we call this content creation. The idea is to come up with topic ideas that will appeal directly to your ideal customers' needs. So I want to share four idea sources that will help you generate more than enough ideas to invest time and possibly money in learning more about so you can share.

Idea Source Number 1 - Write down 10 commonly or frequently asked questions that your ideal customers tend to ask. If this is a business that you are qualified to serve in, it should be pretty simple.

Let me give you a quick secret. You could be learning the business at the same time, in real time, and using these same content creation skills to attract a significant size of the market. When you teach, you literally learn twice.

Most people in any business end up complacent and never learning anything new for years. But when you use this method to create thousands of connections and digital agents for prospects before getting to see your offer, you will remain at the top of your game.

Idea Source Number 2 - For this one, come up with and write down 10 questions you would advise an ideal prospect to ask your competitors. Of course, you want to make sure these are questions and problems that your content and products have answered and solved.

Idea Source Number 3 - Identify 10 common problems that your ideal prospect faces. It doesn't have to be directly linked to the problems that your product solves.

But I was hoping you could do it because the information you will provide in the content will actually serve an audience. But in addition to that, you may end up creating a tangible and usable solution if the piece of content is attracting a big enough audience.

Last but not least…

Idea Source Number 4 - Invest time to learn about 10 common mistakes that an ideal prospect would or could make and share each one as a piece of content. In addition to that, share tips on how to avoid mistakes.

I've used this same method of connection to build my business and the good thing about it; you can verify. At press time, about 840 myEmpirePRO web pages are resulting and indexed on the Google Search Engine Results Page. (THE SERP).

And on another web property that I am building with my wife, LOLAandOLA.com, about 1,370 web pages of content are resulting and indexed. I am not even talking about other search engines such as Yahoo, Bing, and many others that thrive off of picking up your content and connecting it with potential prospects worldwide for free.

65.78% of our audience at myEmpirePRO in the last 28 days from press time are coming from the United States. 13.46% are coming from China. 3.77% are coming from Canada. The audience or traffic was connected from 48 different countries.

The beauty about digital marketing is the fact that you are also collecting tons of data with the various default activities of setting up and running these campaigns. That's why I am able to share these results with you. In fact, you can check it yourself.

All you have to do is place this string 'site:' before any site with no spaces between them and search. For example, a simple search of **'site:myempirepro.com'** will show the top of the SERP (search engine results page), and it will show you how many pages have been indexed from the site.

What about YouTube? We've published 1,304 videos, and they are all working in our favor to connect more prospects to our hub. All these digital agents are not built overnight, and they don't need to be built overnight.

In fact, all it takes is one good piece of content to create a $10,000 day. But that also depends on what you are selling and your business model. You just never know what answered question would resonate with someone's deep pain. The more you put out there, the better.

In order to execute a massive connection, KLT, and brand equity campaign, you have to create a main online hub where everyone comes to from all these different sources you will be putting out there. The main hub is a content management system, and I recommend good ol' WordPress.

On the internet today, we have websites designed to simply display information, like the Toyota website from 1995 in that story I shared with you earlier. But we also have websites designed to manage content, users, and users' information databases. We call them a content management system (CMS).

You have two options. You can build and code your CMS with all the bells and whistles that make it a robust system to create millions of dollars in online transactions from scratch. The second option is what I recommend, which involves leveraging existing tools and systems that allow you to customize with add-ons to perform even better than systems that are built from scratch.

Which option do you think you should go with? Okay. That wasn't a trick question. It's a simple question, and it has a simple answer: to leverage tools and systems so that you can make money as soon as possible.

At press time, WordPress powers a little more than 40% of the websites online and their content management system. I recommend it because it works just like the iPhone and Android phones, and it's an open source that allows vendors to continue to add additional code features, many of which you can leverage for free.

That's why I recommend WordPress, in addition to the fact that I personally use it to manage my content marketing campaign. But there are also two different kinds of WordPress websites.

1. Fully hosted WordPress website which is hosted at wordpress.com and
2. Self-hosted WordPress website means you are in full control of the features you attach to it.

You will understand later many reasons why it is better to go with option number 2, in addition to the fact that you can control how you are branded online.

Brand control is non-negotiable as we move into the future because competition is increasing. With a brand you create, you will eliminate a significant number of your competition because of brand loyalty, the same effect that Apple has on its customers. I recommend that you set up your self-hosted WordPress hub with the company at this link for less than $10 per month.

www.myEmpirePRO.com/hosting

All of these you've learned thus far without setting them up as a system is just another job that will occupy your life with redundant activities and minimum wages. So in the next chapter, we will talk about changing these new insights into an automated system that takes your prospects on a journey from discovery to conversion and a happy customer.

By now, you are understanding slowly that setting up a website is just the bare minimum of digital marketing. Most websites on the internet are a ghost land. No one is visiting them, much less initiating a transaction.

So there is a distinct difference between a digital marketer and a website designer or developer. The former is a minimum of a 6-figure career as a job and a 7-9 figure income when you use this skill as an entrepreneur. The latter is darn near a minimum-wage job.

With systems, you can scale a campaign beyond what's possible when all you've got are linear operations involving humans at every segment. You will learn about different segments in a customer's life cycle and how systems can scale from 10 customers to 100 and to 1,000 customers being served simultaneously.

The last thing I want you to do is know all this cool stuff only to get stuck behind a laptop for 16 hours a day. While I definitely want you to understand the concepts that make this work, I will be sharing with you how to set, forget and collect on a regular basis leveraging the concept of systems.

CHAPTER 5

The System

I have to go back to 1997 to make this make sense. It looked like I was going to be at home for a while before heading to some kind of higher education, so I decided to take a 3 months introductory course in computers.

The first thing I learned that continues to show up for the next 25 years for me… What was it? It was input, CPU (central processing unit), and output, the three basic parts of a personal computer. Since then, there have been multiple versions of that.

But it allowed me to understand at a fundamental level what value a computer brings to our lives from a system standpoint. And I continue to believe in every aspect of life that the best part about humans is the ability to build systems that work even when we can't.

A system is a set of parts or principles that work together to create the desired outcome. The outcome can actually be a part of the system or a recursive input into the system to create an even better outcome or output.

And Like I said, the first thing I learned about computers is their 3 basic parts, namely input devices such as the keyboard, the CPU, which contains the memory for storage and processes information coming through the input devices, and lastly, the output devices such as the monitor to see visuals of the work being performed by the computer or to store information on external storage.

The external storage device that was popular back in 1997 was a floppy disk. While you can use it to store information digitally as an output from the CPU, it is often inserted back as input into the CPU for additional, better, and improved output.

In this chapter, we are going to explore the concept of systems and how it applies at micro and macro levels when it comes to digital marketing.

But in the previous chapter, we discussed "The Connection" in many dimensions. We talked about frame of reference. It's a concept that we will revisit again because this whole thing is about the customer journey. And your ability to take them on an experience is a big determining factor in the level of success you can create.

As I said in the last chapter, many businesses go back and forth between futuristic marketing and old-school media that doesn't work anymore, such as newspapers and yellow books ads. Remember, this is about "The Persons," the people, and catering to your identified audience.

95% of businesses are already going to fail within their first five years. Feel free to attribute that terrible result to a lack of connection between "The Value" and "The Persons." It just makes sense, right?

We covered the idea of pre-framing your prospect's mind so that the natural order of action is to create an order; buy your offer. Hopefully now, you understand that people need to "feel" like they know, like and trust you as part of the pre-framing. And getting people to convert to customers, clients, deals and partners start to feel almost effortless.

Very importantly, we covered a tool that helps us create a spider web of these agents and connections worldwide. Do you recall the content management system?

The CMS, right? My favorite CMS, WordPress, controls 40% of the CMS market share.

That is a good thing because of the ever-evolving nature of everything digital. So like typical software, there are constant and seamless updates of bells and whistles to make your customers' experiences super-cutting edge. In this era, you, a business owner or digital marketer, cannot afford to operate on stale systems.

With that being said, let's get into systems when it comes to digital marketing and digital-based businesses. You guessed it right. It starts with an input.

In 2009, I was introduced to multilevel marketing and direct sales. The truth is that it wasn't just about finding customers. In fact, the majority of the income came from building a team. Being the self-motivated person I've always been, I got to work immediately, and I recruited my brother into my downline.

The idea behind the business model leverages people's immediate circle of influence to first… sell the business opportunity to and then second sell them products if they are not interested in building the business.

My brother figured out quickly that the main input into the business model was people. The owners of these multilevel marketing businesses, such as Amway, Herbalife, TransAmerica, Primerica, etc., simply need people.

But there is a problem. Sure, we can probably go through the contacts of our smartphones and find 100 people, and the issue is that we usually haven't connected with these people in a long time. So even though they are people, they are not necessarily suitable inputs for the business model. Hence many of the reps get frustrated until they quit the business.

Also, we are talking about a business model that requires face-to-face sales skills. While a lot of the leaders and trainers in that industry continue to tell their teammates that sales are not involved, nothing could be further from the truth. The reality is that money is expected to exchange hands with an opportunity, a business opportunity, or at least a product.

So even the second part of this business system is flawed, with mostly non-capable business owners and processes that aren't updated for the digital era. No arguments. If it's working for you, keep doing what you are doing because it works, right?

In the last few years, many multi-level marketers have transferred the same not-so-professional strategies to social media. All they do is pitch everyone, by *"throwing everything at the wall and hoping that something sticks."*

Most other types of businesses make the same mistake; not identifying a suitable input necessary with well-thought-out processes and systems that can operate even when humans are not involved. So if the main person gets sick or encounters an emergency, operations will shut down immediately; just an over-glorified and undercompensated after 9-5 job.

If your marketing needs your attention constantly in order to continue filling the pipeline, it cannot be working competitively in these times. Back in the days, the only call-to-action on commercials was the phone number which meant someone had to pick up the phone on the other end. If they don't pick up, you've lost money.

When that happens enough time, it can take your business out effectively, becoming the 95% in 5 years failure stat member. Since then, marketing has evolved not to involve the need of humans to receive these messages.

Back in 1998, there were the famous 900 numbers all over television commercials. Not only did these numbers actually charge the callers a fee that shares royalties with the business on the other end, but automated answering machines also picked up the phone.

So the more your marketing involves humans, the higher the cost of marketing will be because of the cost of human resources and time. Systems can still involve human time, but the idea is to minimize that particular variable in your marketing, therefore, reducing or offsetting marketing costs dramatically.

In the same way, we have inputs, central processing units (CPU), and outputs as the three basic parts of a personal computer, your marketing operation must identify the inputs, processes, and outputs. A business can no longer just be a business; it must be a business **"system."**

And that means you are able to take a walk without the risk of the business shutting down.

There are multi-layers of systems in any given business, and one of them is obviously the marketing system. To further break this down, I want to borrow some ideas for what I learned in Project Management Professional (PMP®). Surprise… surprise… They use similar concepts to break down projects.

Projects have multiple processes, which are subsets of systems. Each process has its own inputs, tools and techniques (TT), and outputs. For short, you might encounter ITTO if you are into project management. The reality is that each campaign is like a project, especially if it has an end date or predetermined and desired end results.

Back in the days, you might just worry about the input and the output as a business owner while the process in between them is handled by a marketing agency. But in this digital era, any individual with a Facebook or Google account has access to millions of target audiences.

In many ways, marketing agencies are still very useful. In fact, you can inquire more at www.myEmpirePRO.com/services about our marketing agency services. But the point is that the business owners are much more involved in the middle component of a marketing system, the processes, at least at a consulting and services level.

Throughout the rest of this book, we will get into more detail about the different components of a marketing system and campaign. My focus right now is just to highlight the importance of executing the marketing campaign of a business, product, or service like a system.

What it does is that it removes the guesswork and allows you to replicate more of what's working and delete whatever is not working. You will be able to scale your business without and simultaneously eliminate human error in that process.

We will elaborate on two metrics later, namely, ACV and LCV. They stand for Average Customer Value and Lifetime Customer Value, respectively. These are the KPIs

(Key Performance Indicators) that allow you to test offers in different types of ways.

Do you know the average or lifetime customer value of your business? If you do not know this number, you can't scale the business because it's directly an indication that you don't even know your business.

It's very simple. Over a period of time, divide your total revenue by the number of customers; the product is your average customer value. Lifetime is simply the same number over the lifetime of your business.

You can't properly measure these numbers when you don't have systems that **systemically** make offers in a particular sequence based on a customer's journey into and through your offers. And the last thing you want to try is manually measuring and calculating these important numbers. You will lose track.

Here are some examples of systems that allow you to measure your ACV and LCV so that you can know when and how much to invest in marketing campaigns.

Funded Proposal - Anytime you have an offer, product, or service for the marketplace, think of it as a proposal. You are proposing a solution where the buyer has the agency to decide whether to buy or not.

An average business does not have a choice of entering a profitable zone until 5 years after launch. But what if you can create and position offers that will fund your marketing campaigns upfront?

I am not talking about your main offer or core product. When you implement a funded proposal in your business, all the sales of your core product become pure profit. There is a self-liquidating or tripwire offer that funds your marketing campaigns and most especially, customer list-building. Once you have these customers in your funnel, it's easier to sell your main core product to them.

Hopefully, you have the skills to orchestrate a sequence of offers that naturally ascends your customers through your sales funnel.

Sales Funnels - What is a sales funnel? Simply put, it's the journey that you have designed for your customers to go from discovering your business to sales conversion. More often than none, one sale conversion is not enough to make your business profitable.

Like I said earlier, if your business falls within the range of an average business, you won't be in profit for 5 years or never. By designing a sales funnel that ensures profit upfront and funding your marketing campaign as soon as possible, your business will legally print money.

If you are able to make $1.10 every time you spend a dollar in any given year, you are effectively printing money. How would you like it if you were able to spend $22,787.30 and generate a revenue of 49,059.80 all in less than 3 years? That's a 60+% return on investment (ROI).

All of that happened and even more so during the covid pandemic. It dramatically recession-proofs your business. By the way, that's a true story and you can replicate that result, especially when you understand the power of upselling funnels.

Upsell Funnels - Have you ever been asked, *"would you want fries with that?"* after buying something off McDonald's basic entry menu? (It's no longer called the dollar menu, right? Thanks to inflation).

What about *"would you like 2 apple pies for $1.99?"* That is a real example of an upsell offer. With digital marketing, you can create and position offers after a first offer purchase (the tripwire offer) has been initiated.

In addition to that, you can offer a down-sell to customers that say no to an offer if the reason for declining is likely to be cost. For example, you made an offer of $4,997 inside an upsell sales funnel, and your customer clicks "no thanks."

As soon as they click on that, they can be redirected to an offer with fewer features at the price of $2,497. Sometimes, you can also offer a payment plan. By doing this, you can secure a sale and additional revenue that would otherwise not have happened if you were presenting to total strangers.

Check out this web-based sales funnel and list-building system if you want a free trial of marketing automation with your digital marketing efforts. Keep in mind that we are talking about systems.

www.myEmpirePRO.com/salesfunnel

Inside the system are processes such as email marketing, autoresponders, audience segmentation, customer engagement, audience growth, and more to boost your online sales.

Typically, digital marketers use multiple tools to execute all these different techniques. In fact, there are more than enough techniques, and if you are not careful, that's a negative thing. It can be hard to stay focused.

Once you get the ball rolling and you fully understand this as a system, one tool can execute everything. Sometimes, you might have different aspects of your business with their own sales processes. But ideally, it's better to keep all your processes in one system, especially if you are new to digital marketing.

The shiny ball syndrome is real, and distractions are extremely costly. I know because I am speaking from experience. There are many different types of systems implementable for digital marketing. But the best ones for what should be obvious to you after the next chapter starts with list building; audience growth.

If you have to spend money for every unit of discovery, your business will likely go broke. The reason why all the best businesses you know today create smartphone apps to engage you and offer rewards is to build and engage their audience on a regular basis. The idea is to create and boost more sales.

So in the next chapter, we are going to dive into list building. Have you ever heard the saying, "the money is on 'the list?" I've heard some people try to dumb this down, but they are also usually trying to sell something else. List building as the front end of your sales funnel system is undefeatable and we will be talking about it.

What is a system without at least an input? Useless right? The sales funnel as a system is a beautiful beast, but without making sure that you are feeding the beast, it's all pointless. In addition to that, we will be talking about quality vs. quantity. We will also talk about all the different list-building forms and how it has evolved before my eyes since 2009.

There have been many moments over the years when I derailed from this ideology. Yes, I agree. It's still an ideology, but yielding away from it has cost me millions in losses. Don't make the same mistake.

There is a space from a mindset standpoint that it might seem like you can get quicker results starting your sales funnel system by asking for money from strangers. Remember, people need to feel like they know, like and trust you.

Do you remember the KLT factor and brand equity? How much more when you are able to fund your marketing campaigns simultaneously on the front end?

And what if the output of your sales funnel system is customers who can't wait to buy more from you? Then your output becomes a recursive input for your system, making it faster to scale your business. They can also buy from partners through you.

CHAPTER 6

The List

So in April 2009, I was fresh out of the real estate crash, and I was attempting different things. I built an online mall. I discovered affiliate marketing for the first time. And I tried to use the concept to invent a cashback mall. Today, you can see many cashback opportunities with credit cards and retail reward programs attached to different websites.

Anyway, I paid a couple of hundred dollars for a home study course, and I learned about the Google Ads platform for the first time. Back then and up till not too long ago, it was called Google Adwords.

The concept was simple. All I had to do was find a product on an affiliate network that paid a commission for generating sales. In order to generate sales, all I had to do was give my special trackable link to a prospect and I would earn a commission if a sale was generated as a result of clicking my trackable link.

In my mind, at that moment, I had hit the jackpot. So I searched through the product affiliate network and found an e-book on generating real estate fortunes, and I could relate because the previous few years before that... that was my life; real estate.

I decided to set up my first Good Adwords campaign and in about 5 minutes, Google had charged my credit card for $700. A $47 sale was generated. I panicked, and I turned the damn campaign off immediately.

So let's do the math. $700 minus $47 is equal to $653 in a net loss. But I also generated the million-dollar lesson I am about to share with you right now. Since then, I've used it so many times as a guide whenever I'm setting up any type of campaign, especially with digital marketing.

The last chapter discussed "the system", input, tools, techniques, processes, and outputs. We talked about how important it is to build a campaign in a self-sustainable way so that you do not have to be enslaved to make it work.

To a large extent, humans are still needed to test, run and scale successful digital marketing campaigns. But ideally, you want to set it up in a way that humans are only needed for the setup and data analysis for scaling growth.

And with "humans in this respect, I am not talking about the human prospects or audience of the campaign. I am talking about the digital marketer or the entrepreneur seeking to build the audience and subsequently sales generation for a business.

We discussed the fact that many digital marketing tools are available in the marketplace. In fact, the majority of them will be described as systems. And frankly, they are all systems in their own right as long as an input, a process, and an output are identifiable.

All processes can, in fact, be described as a system. But I need you to understand that each of your digital marketing campaigns or projects is a standalone system that involves multiple processes hopefully with trackable and measurable inputs and outputs.

This is how to turn a complex process into super simple and easy to understandable and implementable execution. Suppose I come to you and ask you to break down a brand awareness campaign for a new version of the

Toyota Highlander on the Meta/Facebook Advertising platform. In that case, you can now draw a plan on a piece of paper in an effort to understand what the inputs and the outputs would be.

What resources are available, and what are the desired outcomes of the campaign? It's a mindset shift. In addition to that, you will increase the chances of better outputs from the campaign just by having a plan.

But there is a major problem. The gentleman who was the actual instructor of the Google Adwords home study course actually described different types of campaigns.

He talked about the first one which is a sales generation campaign. It involved setting up a campaign that landed on a sales presentation page as soon as you clicked the ad on the search engine results page (THE SERP).

In digital marketing, there is something called "the bounce."

What is the bounce?

A bounce happens when a user clicks a marketing message to land on your website but the landing page is the only page they viewed. In real life, they typically don't like what they see, and they click the 'BACK' button to go back to the SERP.

So when you set up a campaign with traffic or clicks as the objective, a bounce means you just lost money equivalent to the cost of that one click. The ultimate objective is to create sales. What are the chances that a sale will be generated from any given click on your ad?

From decade-long experience, it's 10% or less, no matter how good your sales copy is.

So how did I end up with a $700 bill and a $47 sale which entitled me to only 50% commission ($23.50), by the way? I generated tons of clicks, most of which turned out to be bounced for many reasons. Each one of the clicks cost me a certain amount of money.

For the sake of simplicity, let's assume that each click costs me $1.07. So that means (700 divided by $1.07) 654 clicks on the ad generated that $700 bill. After 5 minutes, only one sale was generated. That would be one sale divided by 654 clicks and then multiplied by 100%. That's equal to 0.15% sales per click rate.

At that rate, how long will it take to break even if I ever do? As you can see, I am probably better off building a business than the traditional route.

The instructor shared that the second type of campaign in the home study course was a list-building campaign. In this type of campaign, the ultimate objective is no longer sales. Okay. It is sales for the business but not just "sales." The ultimate objective is maximizing profits.

As a newbie in digital marketing, I was super excited about the idea of working from home or from the beach with a laptop generating money on demand. Who doesn't want that? So my natural instinct was to choose the clicks generation campaign objective camouflaged as the sales objective. At the back of my mind, a lot of clicks would turn to sales since they had interest.

I went ahead and set up a clicks or traffic generation campaign without thinking things all the way through and properly. It was a short-sighted strategy, and it burnt me badly. Let me explain.

In that example that I gave earlier, there were (654 minus 1 sale) 653 prospects that I paid actual money to attract to my landing page with the sales presentation, right? Those people had an actual interest, as evidenced by their actions, and they actually clicked the ad.

But if I wanted to attract them again, I would have to spend another $700 and there is no guarantee that I would get them to buy the product. In fact, if the number worked out the way it did before, I would now be ($1,400 minus $47) $1,353 in the hole; net loss. It's getting worse right?

Every time I want to sell a product to these people that I've identified as having interest, I would have to spend money and potentially lose more money. This is not turning out to be a profitable venture so far right?

From the previous chapters, you learned that 85% of people make buying decisions based on emotions and justify them with logic later. You also learned that they are more likely to buy from you when they feel like they know, like, and trust you. Do you still remember the KLT factor and brand equity? So we know that the less exposure to your brand is, the more unlikely it is for the prospect to buy.

With list building as the objective of a front-end digital marketing campaign, you are now able to remarket to prospects with established interests without spending more money. As a business owner, of course, and hopefully, you understand the principles of sowing in order to reap. You are going to have to spend money to make money.

But it's obviously better if you can spend money one time to attract targeted prospects with a certain level of interest rather than for every single time you need to attract them to your website. If the main objective on the front end is to capture their contact information into a list, you can then contact them more times with your paid offer after the initial contact.

Let me ask you a question. Which action do you think would be easier to get your website user to take on their first encounter with you? Is it easier to get them to pull out their credit card to buy a product, or is it easier to get them to give out their contact information in order to receive a free sample or additional information on a solution they are already interested in?

Your guess is as good as mine. Is it probably easier to get them to spend no money right? ....especially if they don't feel like they know, like, or trust you yet. Since you are capturing contact information, you can put a lot of focus on building that KLT factor or brand equity until they feel comfortable buying, which is the ultimate goal.

It's also better like this because of the magnitude of the impact you are leaving on your prospects long before they decide to do business with you and long after. They are even more inclined to refer more business to you. You are maximizing the output of your marketing input and resources simply to understand the power of list building as a front-end digital marketing campaign objective.

Think of it as a follow-up strategy in a traditional business model. Follow-up is another form of marketing, except that it will now cost you almost nothing and a lot less effort to convert a prospect to a customer. This will massively offset your marketing cost.

There are many more benefits to list building as a core digital marketing strategy but let me leave you with these two benefits.

Sales on Demand - When you diligently build a list of prospects, you can send a quick email just like that and have your mortgage for the month paid.

Community Building - In addition to the heightened need to build brand equity due to competition, it's also important to build a community around your business. List building makes it super simple to drive prospects into a discussion group where you can even get better opportunities to develop new ideas into more products.

The first step to list building is to find or create a free and valuable offer. This book is an example of a free offer that we use to generate leads and build our list. As we were marketing this book to 17 million people to download for free, this comment was left on one of the ads.

"Just Think...who would PAY for an advert and THEN give you somthing for FREE...Scammers are clever people....."

And this was my reply….

"False. People who created value, like a book, that you probably will never create and use it to generate leads for potentially more business... aka... opportunity to give more value. Why are you triggered by the idea of people making money? You should see a therapist. The book is free and that's that. Drink some water."

Now that was a little harsh for a reply. I guess that person caught me on a good day because we generally delete negative comments. It's just pointless to reply to people who have made up their minds not to do business with you. But you get the gist.

It might be a product sample that you are offering your target audience. It's free and they get to have a taste of enjoying your product or services. You might have seen examples of products being offered in exchange for just the cost of shipping.

Surprise… surprise. When you pay for the shipping and handling, your contact information which includes your physical shipping address, is also captured all legally. That's how you print money with digital marketing.

As I said, I have used the same method to build my business over the years. But I have to be 100% honest with you. I've had moments of non-profitable greed when I attempted to sell to strangers without getting to know them and, more importantly, getting them to know me; brand equity.

That behavior has cost me millions of dollars in a net loss. When you are in a desperate place, it's easy to fall back on natural "common sense-based" instincts, which assume that a good offer is good enough. A good offer is absolutely a necessity. But so is timing for your prospect and audience. It's not always the right time for your prospect, but you must set up and position your digital marketing campaigns in a way that the timing is always right for your campaigns to sell to a prospect who is ready to buy.

Go to your favorite social media platform and click on one of the ads you see. They typically have "sponsored" as a label next to them. What that means is that someone is paying money to the platform to target you with an offer.

Click on about 10 ads and observe how they attempt to capture your contact information; email, phone number, physical address, etc. Also, pay attention to what type of free offer they are exchanging for it. Make sure it's not a brand you've seen before because it most likely wouldn't be a first-time or front-end exposure ad. It's probably a remarketing campaign.

Speaking of remarketing campaigns, in recent years, you can capture people into ad platform custom audiences once they take certain actions or engage with your ad. Although I wouldn't count on just that as a form of list building but it's doable if your marketing budget is big enough for that type of risk.

However, if you lose that ad account which can happen, you might lose the opportunity to be able to market to the audiences you build in it. That's very costly.

By the way, we use the same system I mentioned in the last chapter for list building, and you can check it out at www.myEmpirePRO.com/listbuilding. The ultimate goal here is not just to make sales but to maximize profits. Some of the easiest sales you will make will be from existing customers.

It just makes sense because if they received value from doing business with you in the past, they would naturally be inclined to do more business. Having a third-party tool and system to maintain your list and community outside of the ad platform is literally freedom.

Your ad platform's custom audiences (as we will cover later), social media fans, and followers are not as powerful as a list that you nurture and maintain independently. And that's why I recommend a third-party tool that has its own embeddable web form to capture the contact information marketing automation feature to engage and convert prospects into customers, clients, and deals.

I know that I mentioned earlier that one tool could handle so much more than one process. But it is important to separate features on the advertising platform from your list-building system as a form of security and risk mitigation. You don't want to have all your fruits in one basket.

So it is not necessarily smart to leave all the processes from lead to sales generation on one platform. Platforms do collapse, and account profiles can also be banned, shadow banned, and deleted.

In the next section of Digital Marketing Certified, we are going to dive into performance and how to track and monitor it. There are way too many businesses that have no way of ensuring growth and quality in their processes. At the end of the day, it's a competitive marketplace.

Your prospects will spend that money with or without you selling to them. Some other smarter or wiser, direct or indirect competitor will collect that money from them. It might as well be you, right?

To ensure growth from quarter to quarter, you must measure your digital marketing performance across a few dimensions.

SECTION 3

THE PERFORMANCE

CHAPTER 7

The Data

In 2010, I was in a partnership with my brother, and we thought we could make things move a little faster by growing the business.

The New Jersey Northeast Corridor train line travels all the way through our neighborhood from the greatest city in the world, New York City, to the state capital city, Trenton.

So many professionals get on and off this train all week during rush hours daily. These were the types of people we wanted as prospects for the business we were trying to build. So we thought, why not print a bunch of flyers and give them out to all the people coming off the train at 5:45 pm in the evening? Great idea, right?

No, it wasn't. Let me explain. First of all, it was a gross assumption on our part that most people ever want to be sold unsolicited products, even if it's free, and it's a red flag at best.

As they collected the flyers from us, which seemed like it was done out of pity, they dumped them in the next visible garbage.

I understood it but damn, it hurt. Not only did we spend money on printing those flyers, but we also spent time and, even worse, a lot of emotional energy anticipating success.

Anyway, we did not get a single person from that terrible marketing to sign up. I don't believe it was particularly because of the marketing channel. I think it was more so because there was no focused way of tracking the success or some type of progress from this activity, at least for us at the time.

We just wanted to get the words out as soon as possible. But oftentimes, that's the mindset of people who lack strategy. Marketing with no strategy? You might as well grab a lighter and burn down your money.

So we were talking about the list in the last chapter, right? You learned about the mistake that has cost me millions of dollars over the years. By the way, I continue to have urges to mess with the same mistakes.

You learned that the timing is not always right for your prospect, but you must set up in a way that the timing is always right for you to serve when they are ready.

How do you do that? It's as simple as serving your prospect the old-fashioned way by serving first in exchange for their contact information. That gives you the power to re-engage and remarket to them at a lesser cost.

Your business's original discovery and exposure to prospects cost you marketing dollars, right? But when you focus on list building as the main objective of your business's front-end campaign, it dramatically offsets your marketing cost.

In that chapter, you learn the various ways to ensure that you are capturing leads (contact information) even when you are offering free shipping and handling. The ultimate goal is still to capture contact information and build a list of these highly targeted prospects.

This list we are talking about becomes the company's greatest asset since the money comes from only one place; from people.

You learned that it's not just about the data, email addresses, phone numbers, and people's names. It's more so about the fact that the individuals associated with this data have demonstrated high interest in what is being offered.

Remember. You learned that many people would attempt to sell you data online. But they will mostly be selling you useless data of prospects who haven't shown or demonstrated interest in your offer.

At best, you will lose money in these types of activities. There are some hacks around retargeting purchased data online with major advertising platforms, and it's still a gamble.

But I wasn't even talking about that type of data. There is a big problem.

There is nothing worse than getting excited about the extremely profitable opportunities that digital marketing presents and then losing your life savings to Facebook and Google trying to implement them.

Remember that money I lost in 5 minutes? It is even easier to waste resources on marketing that doesn't collect data. If you are not tracking the present status and performance of your marketing campaigns, how could you possibly create a plan to get you to the desired destination?

To jump on an advertising platform is one of the easiest things to do nowadays, and it's user-friendly. But again, it's just as easy to lose money. In fact, the more buoyant you are, the easier it is for you to lose money.

On the flip side, if you are broke, you would be watching every penny, which takes your focus off collecting big enough samples to create a profitable business.

Most people initiating digital marketing campaigns might set up a $5 per day ad campaign and leave it running. By the time they get charged $150 on the 30th day, they suddenly realize that these advertising platforms know exactly what they are doing. They are not playing. They will take your money in a heartbeat.

At press time, Meta Platforms Inc (formerly Facebook) is worth USD $372.52 Billion, and Alphabet Inc (The owner of Google) is worth a whopping USD $1.29 Trillion. They don't need your money if you are not going to make money from advertising with them.

But also, they continue to make serious money because digital marketing works for many companies. Data is one factor that separates the losers and the winners in digital marketing.

Every marketing activity creates some type of data. The question is, are you collecting that data?

In our flyer story that I shared with you earlier, we couldn't tell you how many flyers we printed and how many ended up in the garbage. That's a major problem.

It's not enough to just plan and execute a digital marketing campaign. You set a smart goal from inception, right? But there are also so many stops before the destination, which is probably a net profit.

How much did you spend on the campaign, and how much was the revenue that was generated from it? That's too wide of a gap to wait on executing in order to track and ensure success.

When a prospect encounters your ad for the first time, that is a discovery. An impression was created. That's literally the first goal that we want to track.

How many impressions did your business, message, or ad receive in the last 28 days, last 7 days, and yesterday? The answer is data that we want to continue to collect because the more it is, the better, all things being equal. It means exposure.

When you are a novice in marketing like my brother and I was, you are marketing, but you are not collecting data to measure success. And if you do, you are not doing so unless an actual sale has happened.

That's not good enough because you are not able to troubleshoot and diagnose without involving so much emotion. But when you start collecting meaningful data as early as when an impression is created for an ad, an image, a copy, or a message, you stand a better chance at tracking performance as early as possible all the way to success.

And even when data indicates an undesirable result, you are able to generate that data much faster and earlier. That also means that you are able to pivot and adjust much earlier in the direction of the results you want to create.

The answer is data and data collection. It's just a fancy way of saying success tracking. With digital marketing, you are able to track micro-levels of success. Unmanaged expectations only lead to disappointments. So it is necessary to have ways to track and measure expectations, goals, and objectives in order to avoid overall disappointments.

Without it, you will keep wasting a significant amount of your resources on marketing activities that not just fail but also leave you with a bad taste in your mouth, kind of like distributing a bunch of flyers that get thrown in the garbage right in front of you.

What if you are tracking how many of those flyers go in the garbage, along with how many calls you get from the ones that were kept? More importantly, are you patient enough to be tracking this data? The more you add yourself physically into the process, the fewer chances that you even know how to track your marketing properly in the digital age.

Tracking these data allows you to identify benchmarks and baselines to track your marketing performance against. It facilitates exponential growth and reduces your chances of entertaining costly distractions across the board.

In business, there is often confusion between methods of performance analysis. Between qualitative and quantitative analysis, which one is better? It depends on who you are asking and their general outlook on data-driven business decisions.

By tracking these numbers, you are better positioned to objectively orchestrate the results you are looking to create from your digital marketing campaigns. The data being collected becomes available for further analysis and competitive advantage, and your competitors will have difficulty matching your performance level.

On the flip side, many emotions are involved and camouflaged as qualitative analysis when you put your heart and soul into a dinosaur and old-school marketing activities. You are telling yourself a lie that will consume your resources and return almost nothing.

So let's break down 7 or 8 of the most important metrics you will encounter consistently when collecting digital marketing performance data over time. The period is typically set as default at "last 28 days". But it can also be "last 7 days", last 90 days, last 365 days, or even lifetime. Let's identify the different metrics.

Impression - This is the number of times a digital creative (content, ad copy, image, video, etc.) is visible to the human eyes.

Users - This is the number of individuals that have seen a digital creative. If one person sees the same content twice, it is counted as one user because it's the same user. On some platforms, the number of users is also called "reach." This metric is also broken down into new and returning users. Ideally, you want both metrics to be increasing.

An increasing number of new users means you are doing a good job at attracting new eyeballs on a consistent basis. And increasing returning users means you deliver highly engaging value, potentially creating repeat customers.

Click - This is the number of times creatives are engaged with a mouse click or mobile's finger or stylus tap that actually redirects a loaded webpage to another.

View or Pageview - While the clicks were mostly concerned about redirecting the user to another webpage, it doesn't always result in a full pageview. Pageview is the metric that measures the number of times a page is fully loaded by a user.

This is called a view of the main creative on the page and is a video that autoplays at a full page load. However, not all page views lead to a video view because some videos are not set to auto-play.

Lead Conversion - This is the conversion metric that measures the number of user contacts that are captured for list building and future follow-up, indicative of higher interest.

Sale Conversion - This conversion metric measures the number of transactions that increase revenue. On some data collection and tracking platforms, a conversion is also called an action or a goal.

Cost - This is the total amount of dollars spent on marketing and advertising. And here is a bonus but probably the most important metric.

Revenue is the total amount of money generated, tracked, or attributed to running a digital campaign.

Presently, we have two main digital marketing projects that I'd love to share with you. These are real-life businesses, and I'd love to share a few examples of data we are collecting with you at press time.

As a matter of fact, two email notifications came in as I was writing this chapter. They usually come in between the 1st and the 3rd day of every month from the Google Search Console team. This report is particularly received for sites that generate organic traffic from Google searches.

So our first main project is myEmpirePRO.com which generated 19,700 impressions and 224 clicks in the whole of the last month. There were also 38 pages with their first impressions ever. That means Google showed these 38 web pages to their users for the first time ever.

New content achievements were also reported, such as the top three growing pages generating more clicks from the search engine results page (SERP) ranking. The top two growing pages generated 5 more clicks than the previous month, and the third runners-up generated two more clicks than the previous month's.

Also, top-performing pages with the highest total number of clicks generated were also reported. The highest-performing page generated 44 clicks, the second runners-up generated 24 clicks, and the third runners-up generated 19 clicks. More data is reported, and a button takes you to the full report hosted on the Google search console.

Our second project is LOLAandOLA.com which generated 24,600 impressions and 519 clicks in the whole the previous month. There were also 15 pages with their first impressions ever. Again, that means Google showed these 15 web pages to their users for the first time ever.

New content achievements were also reported, such as the top three growing pages generating more clicks from the search engine results page (SERP) ranking. The highest growing page generated 10 more clicks than the previous month's, and the second and third generated 8 more clicks each than the previous month's.

Also, the top-performing pages with the highest total number of clicks generated were also reported. The highest-performing page generated 64 clicks, the second runners-up generated 47 clicks, and the third runners-up generated 45 clicks.

We have access to these data and so much more, which means we can track the performance of these digital marketing campaigns. That means we can scale the winners and kill the losers.

This is what I want you to do to start collecting this data set for your digital marketing activities. I want you to set up two tools for your self-hosted web projects. Two tracking tools set is perfect because there is no single tracking tool that is perfect. They all have discrepancies in their collected data.

Google Search Console - These sets of tools and reports help you measure your site's search traffic and performance, fix issues, and make your site shine in Google Search results.

The data sets I shared with you from the monthly reports of our two projects are from that console. It's particularly good for you if you want to invest time and resources into generating organic traffic for the Google search engine.

Simply go to:

https://search.google.com/search-console/

Add your website information, click continue, and follow the instructions to start collecting the data. It's free, like many Google tools and modules. If the interface is a little different by the time you are reading this, just follow the instructions on the screen.

For traffic that we are generating from sources other than organic, we use third-party tracking that helps us measure click data and optimize ads and the whole sales process.

Check it out at: myEmpirePRO.com/clickmagick

It comes with more flexibility if you don't want to depend on the reports from the ad platforms selling your traffic, avoiding conflict of interest.

What do we do with the data we are collecting? How do we leverage them to facilitate growth and better performance? That's what we will cover in the next chapter.

We will get into generating useful information from these data sets to make better business decisions.

Do I need to remind you that 95% of businesses fail within their first 5 years? A lot of the business decisions they make are emotions-driven; that's why. And it gets worse when they notice that they are losing money.

So you will be learning how to generate useful and presentable information that business decision-makers leverage to grow sales and revenue in a digital age.

We might also talk about how to flip information into a $204,555 monthly revenue business. If it sounds too good to be true, it probably isn't. But then that means there is a little probability left to assess, right?

After all, in this digital era, it's all numbers, data, ones, and zeros. If you are not leveraging this opportunity, it's okay. Being average is pretty normal too.

And by the way, you can also overdo data collection and analysis. Overkill does exist when you are obsessed with tracking everything trackable.

Just like in every endeavor, modesty is key when tracking performance at every level of your digital marketing campaigns. Every performance-tracking activity consumes energy and, therefore, must be managed.

CHAPTER 8

The Information

About two years into my digital marketing journey, I discovered high ticket offers as a strategy. I will explain what it means to you in a second. But first, understand it's probably going to be the defining demarcation between suffering and thriving for your bottom line.

I had managed to become a top digital sales producer on a few platforms, but it also felt like I was working too hard to make $30 commissions. To be honest, I was a little spoiled. I often woke up to $219 commission notifications, sometimes more and sometimes less.

Till today, I still get random sales commission notifications from work I did years ago. But I wanted more. I came from the real estate world, where I cashed up to $82,000 in one deal. I knew I had to bring 10X that type of value in order to make that type of money on one single transaction.

So I decided to create an offer with a $4,997 price point for the community I had built and sold a $47 offer to.

There are about '107' $47 in one $4,997. Even though I had packaged an offer with 1,000X value, I still had a little fear whispering in my left ear.

In fact, one of the first pieces of feedback I got while delivering the sales presentation was extremely discouraging. It was a random guy in the chat who called me a joke. *"Who is the sucker that will pay you $4,997 for this crap?"* It was scary.

However, that same presentation created 5 sales. Let's do some quick math. 5 sales of a $4,997 offer is equal to $24,985 from one sales presentation.

And the shocking part about that was this. In their application interview, these new customers told me that they had seen the $47 offer, but it was too cheap for them even to take it seriously.

In the last chapter, we explored data in so many ways related to running your business in a digital age. You learned that every activity and process is an opportunity to collect data, right?

How far did it go with respect to an objective? But how far should it go? We covered all these different metrics and data to collect and why we collect them from a visit to a lead and eventually to sales.

We also touched on "views" as a metric when it comes to videos. Videos are powerful ways of connecting with web users. So it is important to collect data as these users watch videos in order to optimize the performance of these videos.

To an extent, digital marketing professionals and business owners do need to be obsessed with collecting data for optimization. But you also learned that modesty is necessary because what's the point of collecting a bunch of data that will never be analyzed, much less used to optimize campaign performance?

Anytime a user visits one of your web properties, value is created, transferred, and distributed. In fact, money is being spent even before people actually initiate transactions as they consume content that ultimately influences transaction initiations.

So since each little mini-steps informs and influences subsequent steps in the user behavior, you learned that we need to collect data to measure to optimize for the ultimate goal.

All clicks matter when it comes to digital marketing. But all views, pageviews, actions, and user behaviors matter even more. So we must collect these numbers (data) because you never know which one is going to turn into a $19,000 sale... or a $42 sale and everything in between.

In addition to collecting these data, we need to analyze and convert them to meaningful **"information."** You would think that I have the confidence to try new things after that 100x revenue story I just shared with you, right? Nothing could be further from the truth. I've also had enough experiences of losing everything because I tried new things.

The negative traumatic memories are a more impactful stronghold on the human mind. I've had to question my own documented abilities and success stories (millions of dollars in production) many times because of fewer bad results. So it's not as simple as that success story might have made it seem.

While I really enjoy the passion I feel from digital marketing activities, I started to feel exhausted with the amount of hours I was unnecessarily spending on minimum wage technical activities. I started craving for opportunities to deliver big results, which I knew I was capable of doing in exchange for bigger fees especially knowing that I had done it before. I can't call this experiment.

But I was also afraid of creating a new offer that could distract me from what was already working. Distraction is real, and it can cost significantly more than what you think when I say that. It's a variable that's often underrated. I feel like I am still a victim of distraction in business. As I said, I am a little traumatized.

As a creative mind, ideas come to me all the time, and I truly believe my personal net worth would be 100 times of what it is right now if I had been able to control my creative urges a little more.

I get bored easily. And boredom can be a sign of a healthy business. Do you feel me on how much of an oxymoron that is?

So I am terrified of trying new ideas when business is working well for me even though the ideas never stop flowing. Some of these ideas could potentially be 100x my revenue even with less effort, but it's a real struggle because I went broke a few times trying new things.

As best practices in marketing, you have to test your way to the results you are looking to achieve. All the data being collected should be collected as you test variables against themselves, at least in 2 variations at any stop in the user or customer experience.

For example, the fear that tends to overwhelm me when it's time to test all these ideas that I get is easily mitigated once I think about them as opportunities to test for. It starts to feel like fun. In fact, testing new ideas and variations is highly recommended.

The issues come when there is no structure to guide certain levels of creative chaos. But that problem is finally solved when you master the art and science of converting data into "information." You can then use the information to decide on scaling the new idea or killing it.

So in my story, all I had to do was to generate a certain fraction or percentage of my traffic (we also call this visits) towards my $47 offer and whatever is left of the generated traffic towards the $4,997 offer for a period of time until I've generated a minimum of 100 visits in total. The idea of the 100 visits is to statistically have enough samples to make a call of the winning variation. The higher the sample visits, the better.

In the case of this example, you collected the clicks data, which is 100 visits. Some analytic tools might call this 100 users or 100 clicks. You also collected 2 additional pieces of data; 2 sales of the $4,997 offer and 19 sales of the $47 offer.

Up until this point, it's all data. But after analyzing these data points, we found that 2 sales at $4,997 are equal to $9,994 for the bottom line, and 19 sales at $47 are equal to $893. With this **"information,"** we can make a business decision accordingly.

This activity of converting data points to meaningful information for the purpose of intelligent business decisions is called analytics. With analytics and the information you get, you can be more objective in your approach to testing new ideas for viability and therefore reduce the overall emotions in the outcome of your digital marketing campaigns.

Remember that digital marketing is all about a user or prospect's journey from the first moment they land on your website until they convert to a customer. One of the many opportunities that digital marketing presents is the ability to track, monitor, and measure user behavior throughout that experience to optimize it.

While the idea is ultimately to optimize for maximized profit, the purpose, also by default, is to make the experience soothing for the user. You want to be able to deliver value not just with whatever the core product is but also with the experience.

You can analyze, and you can report elaborately and also visually. Business decision-makers at the enterprise level will most likely not have time to be digging through so many data points that today's digital analytic tools are able to collect. So these visual representations, after analysis, are necessary.

Data collection, which we covered in the last chapter, is more about the "information in quantity," which is also useless for business decisions. But once it is analyzed and converted to information in reports, it's about "quality information." It can be reviewed quickly by stakeholders.

95% of businesses are still failing within their first five years. One of the many reasons for this is an ever-evolving consumer pattern. Things get older very quickly in the digital age. With digital marketing analytics, there are patterns revealed earlier enough to pivot before it impacts the business negatively.

If you haven't noticed yet, I've used the title of this chapter to simplify the understanding of digital marketing analytics. Analytics is simply a fancy way to describe analysis and reporting of user behavior data as useful, meaningful, and business decision-making "information."

There are 3 types of analysis that we are generally concerned about overall. Some of these terminologies may change and evolve as you continue your digital marketing journey. However, the concept is evergreen.

And the 3 types of analysis are Acquisition, Behavior, and Conversion (ABC). User data is being collected and analyzed in all of these 3 segments of a user's journey on your online properties, such as your website (your main hub) or one of your main nodes, such as your YouTube channel or Facebook page.

1. Acquisition - This is all the data set collected as a measure of how users were initially attracted to your online properties. It measures how many users, new users, and the number of sessions they initiated. As we covered earlier, a user can visit your online properties multiple times. Each time is referred to as a session.

2. Behavior - This data set tracks and measures the users' behavior of your online properties. It's analyzed, reported, and used to optimize for higher engagement, indicating that they are getting the value they came for.

In this phase, the bounce rate *(which is the rate at which users are viewing only one page in a session, an indication of low engagement)*, the number of pages viewed per session on average, and the average session duration *(which is how long they are spending on your properties)* are measured. As you can see, it gets into a little more analysis of the user behavior.

3. Conversion - Then, we have the measurement of the rate at which certain predetermined goals are achieved, and desired actions are taken. We have goals and actions, such as leads generation and sales generation, of course.

For example, at press time, I have pulled out more recent data for the last 30 days of our Google Analytics.

We've acquired 1,042 users, of which 1,020 are new users. 1,031 sessions were initiated. Let's quickly take a closer look before I get into the "behavior" segment.

When you look at the difference between 1,042 users and 1,020 new users, that means only 22 users were repeated users. Already, I don't like that number. At least, I want as close as possible to half of our total users to be repeat and revisiting users.

Hopefully, the readers that this book attracts will help us accomplish that. We will implement additional measures to improve that number, and I will share more inside myEmpirePRO Inner Circle training.

Also, only 1,031 sessions were initiated, and that's barely more than one page viewed by each user. There is art and there is science to improve engagement. But the point of this lesson is showcased in the next set of analyses; **"Behavior."**

In that segment, the reports indicate a 74.48% bounce rate, 1.61 pages per session, and an average session duration of 1 minute and 2 seconds (00:01:02).

Can we use you as an example regarding **"conversion,"** such as leads or sales generation? When you acquired this book, you became a lead for our business. At the very minimum, you gave us your contact information as an indication of interest in digital marketing either as a career or 7 figure side hustle. What do all these mean?

Well... we have a little more confirmation of our first analysis, which is the fact that we need to improve on our engagement level on www.myEmpirePRO.com

The reality *(and I promise... not an excuse)* is that we have been working on this book and a pivot into teaching more of digital marketing as a 6 figure career and 7 figure side hustle. We expect a sharp increase as we release more in-depth training and success stories, which we will share.

The main point of this chapter is to highlight the transition from the last chapter, which was about learning these data points and metrics into using analytics to convert them to business intelligence. And I've just demonstrated that in real-time with our own main hub; www.myEmpirePRO.com

As your first step to setting up analytics for collecting, analyzing, and reporting on user behavior data, you obviously need a main hub commonly known as a website. You also need the website to be self-hosted. It's just a lot more unreliable to use free blogs.

I also recommend that you build this website on a content management system (CMS) called WordPress. There is a very strong reason why WordPress currently powers 43% of websites online, and one of the reasons is that it is easy to set up, plug and play.

With WordPress, you can add and remove features as it automatically updates for free. In this time and digital age, you should already expect that software and apps need regular updates. I'm sure that you notice the same phenomenon on your smartphone mobile apps. Sometimes, it stops you and makes you update before continuing to use it.

WordPress is the material and structure for your online property. While WordPress is a free CMS, the online property (kinda' like a land in real life) and its digital and easy-to-reference address (like www.myEmpirePRO.com) are not free. But they are extremely affordable.

You can be hosted online for as low as $5 per month. Go to www.myEmpirePRO.com/hosting and set up your WordPress-powered website right away. It's quite user-friendly, and that's in addition to the fact that you can chat with live support if you need help.

They will also help you with setting up the Google Search Console for tracking and optimizing organic traffic, and Google Analytics features so that you, too, can start collecting and analyzing user behavior data.

If you'd rather spend money than time on user and customer acquisition of your website and online properties, you might want to check out this third-party analytics tool at www.myEmpirePRO.com/clickmagick. I think they offer a free trial. Don't quote me.

All of these tools are self-explanatory and easy to use, especially if you read this book multiple times, 10-15 times. It's necessary in order to create mastery.

And like I said earlier, we are teaching digital marketing as a 6-figure 9-5 career and also as a 7-figure side-hustle opportunity. It's wild-open, and anyone can participate either as an employee (21+ job opportunities at various levels) for businesses as a digital marketing analyst or 7 figure creator, or messenger as an entrepreneur.

In the next chapter, we will be addressing a major problem. According to ahref.com, 90% of online content and websites get no traffic; ghost-land. No one comes to these websites.

Hopefully, you execute what you've learned today by setting up your own WordPress-powered professional hub online. But the worst thing that can happen is not to figure out how to be in that top 10% that's getting all the online traffic and generating all the money.

If you are not generating consistent traffic of users to your website, there is no data to collect, much less to analyze, report and use to optimize. It's all useless and a waste of resources.

So we will be diving into the four categories of online traffic channels, and then we will break them down to the different "sources" and media. We will talk about the pros and cons of each one. But we also have to reference them to the resources you already have available.

One of the major issues with people that try to implement digital marketing is when they don't realize that they already participate in one shape or form. I am calling that out, and we will leverage your existing activities and sources of traffic online, and then we can build on top of it.

We will also cover the pros and cons of free and paid traffic generation. Some people will hurt their chances of success going after paid traffic, and the same is true for some that will chase after free traffic. We will be breaking that down as we've done with the book up till this point.

CHAPTER 9

The Sources

Let's go back to 2002. A family friend invited my brother and me to his Somerset, New Jersey apartment. He did mention that there would be a presentation of some sort, but I wasn't paying too much mind to it.

Soon enough, we found out it was a life insurance MLM (multi-level marketing) business opportunity presentation. But it was a completely new concept to me. To my surprise, my brother had already been exposed to it.

For some reason, we ended up not signing up, but I don't remember why. I'm sure it had something to do with being broke college kids at the time. It must have been about $200 to sign up but we didn't.

I want to say… something around a few months later, and I was in the NJIT (my alma mater) library studying when I ran into a schoolmate. As a common talking point, I might have uttered something to the effect of "looking to make some serious money." *"Wanna make money?"* He asks. I answered, "yep *."I can show you how to make money fast."* He says. Before I knew it, I found myself at another business presentation at Newark Penn Station.

Less than a week later, I went for full-blown training on how the business worked, where I found out that the "source" of all this money was people, particularly my family and friends. After much thought, I declined to join the business fully. Of course, my schoolmate was disappointed because that was sales commissions being flushed down the drain.

He took the 'L' like a real 'G .'I ended up joining my first MLM in 2009, about 7 years later. The timing was right, I guess. But I was presented again with the idea of my family and friends being the only "source" of life for my business.

I fully understand that money comes from only one source: people, and I learned a long time ago that the revenue you are going to generate in business is already in the hands of someone. So there was no confusion there.

But begging my family and friends like my friend and schoolmate from 2002 did with me seemed like a bad idea.

After all, that traffic leads and business generation strategy didn't work for me. Why would it work on my family and friends? But I managed to recruit my brother into a partnership with me.

Great minds think alike. I was still willing to set up a business presentation at my apartment, and about 22 people showed up. As a businessman with about 3 years of success at the time, selling people to come over and grab free snacks wasn't hard for me.

Out of my 22 guests, only one person signed up. Less than 24 hours later, she called me and requested a refund. I am sure that family and friends as a "source" of business might have worked for many others before and after me. But you can't judge me for concluding that it would probably never work for me.

So after a little bit of research, I stumbled upon the magnetic marketing concept. It was presented to me as attraction marketing and another guru, Mike Dillard, also presented it as magnetic sponsoring. Well, it made too much sense. My brother also confirmed that he had stumbled into this idea while doing his own research.

We signed up for courses, training, and seminars to continue to master this skill set. In one transaction, I spent more than $600, and then it dawned on me. *"I had just given money to a stranger over the internet."* The internet is a new source, and this was an exciting discovery.

If we are going, to be honest, this is about making money because you and I know that we can't afford to run a business without enough revenue to justify it. So when we say "source," we mean nothing can literally happen in digital marketing without talking about **online traffic**.

Exactly how do we plan to attract visits to our websites, webpages, videos, landing pages, and business? It's not enough to set up a website in the middle of nowhere on the internet. In fact, we can't claim that we are talking about digital marketing until we break down online traffic generation.

As I stated earlier on in the book, more than 90% of web pages on the internet get no organic traffic. More gets no traffic at all outside the bots crawling it occasionally to determine if anything is happening over there.

For the most part, most web pages are ghostland. And there is no real excuse for this because we know that Google is sending free traffic, accounting for at least 50% of traffic on the internet as of 2022, and only 15% of online traffic is paid for. So why is your website not actively working as a "source" of new people, leads, deals, customers, clients, and partners for your business?

You are already aware that an average human goes to one place "and one place only" to research, find solutions, and answer problems; the almighty Google. So why isn't that sounding like the source of all the goodies you need to generate from this digital marketing thing?

Forget about researching and all that boring stuff for a second. Where do you go when you are bored and just want to relax and "chill"? Be honest! Isn't it Instagram? Oh! Sorry, I meant to say TikTok.

The good news is that you are in control of how many people you want to visit your websites. All you need is a strong enough desire, and you can get it all set up in no time. I know that most people still assume that generating traffic is a tech-intensive activity.

If you can order to print a pack of 500 business cards to promote your business, you can definitely go through a 3 steps process to set up a simple ad online to generate clicks over to your website. So it's just a matter of desire.

In this time and age, I want to let you know that online traffic generation is a basic skill. Your business simply won't make it if you are not operating at that level. It's the equivalent of swimming against the ocean tide. I would just hope that you are an exception and, in fact, know what you are doing.

There are a few exceptions. For example, some businesses get a steady supply of new clients from their alliances with government agencies and insurance companies. That's fantastic as long as they understand that scalability will be limited.

But my guess is that you are reading this book because you want better control of sourcing your business with new blood steadily. I don't blame you. The internet is where everyone hangs out for leisure or research answers and solutions.

There is no better time to jump on this as an opportunity. Just like many other opportunities that have come and gone, things will evolve with generating online traffic as well.

But you will learn in a bit that you never need to panic about that. If you master the fundamentals, it's a transferable skill for the rest of your life as a marketer and/or an entrepreneur.

Here are a few reasons you need to be in almost full control of how much online traffic comes to your business regularly. First of all, no condition is permanent. And that same concept is true for traffic "sourcing" and generating in of itself. That means even when you fully buy into what I am saying right now, certain sources of traffic won't continue to work forever.

So just as much as you should never count on government contracts and leads to run your business, you should also never count on one traffic source. Therefore it's very much the same reason why you should be in control of how you attract new people and how much new traffic of people you attract steadily.

When you understand this concept, it will suddenly become okay and more affordable for you to make the inevitable mistakes that most people make in their business. Honestly, that's a perpetual contradiction. You simply can't afford to make the mistake of using the hope strategy to generate fresh business and customers.

So I guess I meant to say that you can afford to make mistakes related to conversion rates inside your funnel when you are generating consistent and quality traffic; remember the connection and the system. But those things become useless when you don't prioritize a consistent traffic flow into it.

Have you ever tried to multiply anything by zero? Is the product always zero, right? No perfect sales funnel, connection, or system is falling out of the skies. Never mind what we discussed in chapters 4 and 5.

Suppose you are not generating and attracting consistent traffic through the funnel. In that case, you are not generating any data, as discussed in chapter 7, you can't test, and you can't optimize for maximized profits.

There are four different categories of online traffic sources that we have to further break down in a few minutes, namely organic, direct, referral, and social traffic.

Organic Search Traffic - This is the source of traffic of people searching for particular solutions. When they searched, a search engine result page (SERP) had one of your web pages listed, and they clicked on it and were redirected to your website. A user of your website was generated for your website from organic search traffic.

Direct Traffic - This is traffic sourced from a user who types your website address directly into a web browser that loads your web page from scratch. This user knew the exact web address on the world wide web (www). Most of the traffic generated online is not generated from direct traffic sources.

Most people you give your website address to one time will forget or lose where it is written before they get to a web browser, even though there is a web browser on their smartphone. For the most part, people will be clicking over from some other web page and redirected to your website.

Referral Traffic - This is traffic sourced from other self-hosted websites that manually link to your website. For example, if someone types www.myempirepro.com into a web browser on a device and loads our webpage, that is considered direct traffic. And to be clear, if you are reading this book on a Kindle or PDF file and you click that link directly, that would not be considered direct traffic. That is considered referral traffic since it's a click redirecting from another web-based content.

Social Traffic - As you probably already know, social media is one of mankind's greatest inventions. It consumes and generates so much attention because, in so many ways, it represents entertainment for 4 billion plus people.

So as business owners and digital marketers, we are sharing articles, videos, photos, and more on social media. When users click any of these creatives on social media, generating a redirect to your website, it is considered social traffic. And yes, you probably should be taking advantage of this as a major source of traffic for your website and business.

I am just sharing these categories with you to make it easier to comprehend your experience properly when you do start to execute. So this is not a guarantee that other platforms will categorize traffic sources exactly like this. But it will be somewhat close, and you will be able to generate traffic to your website on-demand after a few minutes of assessment on how any platform's analytics is set up.

Our website www.myEmpirePRO.com at press time generated 43.76% organic search traffic, 26.52% from direct traffic (we have a specific domain name hybrid strategy for that), 2.29% from referral traffic, 1.03% from social traffic (which we can definitely improve on) and 25.14% from "others" all in the last 28 days alone. A total of 1,012 new users.

"Others" traffic sources are simply traffic sources that the robots were not able to categorize properly. Always remember that digital marketing will never be perfect. Nonetheless, it's the closest you will get to perfect marketing.

After the launch of this book, we will be scaling it all up even bigger because what I teach is clearly working. These are real humans with real-life interests and opportunities to serve by stopping by our websites, and we are going to be scaling.

But I want to share www.LOLAandOLA.com traffic sources with you as well. From 1,059 new users in the last 28 days, 77.93% came from organic search, 17.13% came from direct traffic, 0.84% came from social, and 0.74% came from referral traffic.

This is what I want you to do. I want you to step up your traffic generation game. What do you sell right now? How do you make money today? Yes. You do have something that you sell, even if it's just your time by way of a resume.

And the more eyeballs your resume gets, the higher the chances that you will get a new job offer. It gives you more options to exercise, which means you get to set your own prices in the marketplace. Isn't that empowering?

It's easy to look at everything I've been sharing with you as digital marketing. But it might have been harder for you to relate it to what you sell today. It doesn't have to be. Just simply use "eyeballs" on your resume, products, and service interchangeably with "traffic" or the "source." Then it should start to make sense.

Starting today, start relating with social media and the search engines like a producer and not another consumer. As I told you earlier, there will be more than 4 billion social media users in the year 2022. Obviously, there is more than enough supply of consumers because the whole human race is not even up to 8 billion people.

More than half of us are just consuming social media in general. What if you learn and master step-by-step how to produce social media? Are you fully and cognitively aware of the magnitude of opportunity that is when you find the value you can bring into today's social media marketplace?

There is something that you do effortlessly, but that thing is also extremely valuable to someone either hanging out on social media right now or actively searching for that same exact solution online. That is probably the value your employer recognizes, but they are paying you only 1% of its worth. And I don't blame your employer.

It's time to get your talent, products, and services in front of the people that are most likely going to value them appropriately. That's why in the next chapter, we will be breaking down "the structure."

We are getting closer and closer to executing these multi-million dollar proven concepts for you and your business, even if you don't already own a business.

Only a handful of people will do it. But that's the point. The scarcity of "YOU Inc" is precisely "the source" of your fortune. If you don't stop, I won't stop, not only until I finish writing this book but also until you become a success story from this book.

In the next chapter, I am going to share with you some more sources of the right people. And I will share the fundamentals that work on any platform for setting up and scaling out a 7 figure digital marketing campaign.

CHAPTER 10

The Structure

Early 2005, Sheraton Hotel, Woodbridge, New Jersey… after seeing an ad inside the newspaper Star-Ledger, I showed up to an event where a gentleman was presenting. I purchased his $300 course, and I consider it the best foundation I could have ever had when it comes to running a successful business, and here is why.

The course was basically a slapped-together black-and-white copy made from some sort of 1967 xerox machine. But the content is majorly responsible for the success I've had to date because it started with direct response marketing particularly targeted at a specific pre-defined audience.

But I have to tell you. I think I've come to really appreciate that training even more in recent times. However, because of my lack of experience, I spent years testing out different ideologies that don't put marketing first over the years. After taking account and counting the blessings and the failures, I have concluded that I was, in fact, lucky to have taken that training earlier on in my career.

In fact, it doesn't even matter that I had derailed quite a few times from this concept of purpose and people-driven marketing. It's just so powerful to drive massive success at any moment that I've decided to return to the foundation. The foundation is just as important as the "structure," if not more important.

A few times over the years, I've failed at setting up the "structure" sustainably because of many reasons. One of the main reasons is the fact that stable structures are boring. But at the end of the day, they work. Isn't that all that matters?

But I am still human. And by that, I am alluding to the fact that I still get influenced by the "*shiny object syndrome*.*"*You can also call it *the "grass is greener on the other side"* syndrome.

It's an ongoing battle. But I have gotten better and better with this in recent times. It's about making the foundation just as important as the "structure."

In fact, everything we have discussed thus far in this book is the foundation. And I hope that you take it seriously because it's a foolish man who built his house on the sand.

Over the course of this book, we've discussed the goal, the person, the value, the connection, the system, the list, the data, the information, and the sources. In essence, we have broken down all the parts of digital marketing to make it as simple as possible for anyone with a marketable offer to understand.

Back when I started engaging in digital marketing full-time and more, I had to know everything. Actually, I chose to know everything probably because I really do enjoy the art and science of influencing and persuading people. More importantly, it was useful because I was building a business, just as I am still doing today.

There is more structure in the digital marketing industry today. In fact, I just counted more than 20 jobs where you can earn six figures or more. These are skill sets that are primarily responsible for scaling any business.

Today, you don't have to know everything. Sure, you should have an overview-understanding of each of the areas. But if all you want is a job, you can simply pick one of the previous chapters and don't stop your research until you get to the level equivalent of a doctorate degree.

On the flip side, it is important to read this book 10-15 times in order to make the most out of it. Every additional time you read this relatively small book, you will learn something new. But you will have to excuse the fact that I am not your typical scholastic writer.

In the last chapter, the source, we covered the different web traffic channels. But we didn't get too much into the actual platforms and their categories, such as:

- Search Engine Optimization
- Pay-per-Click Advertising
- Social Media Marketing
- Content Marketing
- Email Marketing
- Affiliate Marketing

And many others...

However, we get a little deeper with each one of these traffic sources and media forms inside our flagship 15-week coaching program "Digital Marketing Intensive" (DMi15). Here at www.myEmpirePRO.com , we primarily focused on content marketing through search engine optimization and paid media via Google and Meta (Facebook) ad platforms.

There are many digital marketing and PPC ad platforms to choose from, namely; Google Ads, YouTube Ads (also part of Google Ads), Meta Ads (which used to be Facebook Ads), Instagram Ads (accessible through Meta Ads), Microsoft Ads (which was once called Bing Ads), LinkedIn Ads, Twitter Ads, Pinterest Ads, TikTok for Business, Snapchat for Business, etc. Each and every one of those ad platforms tends to follow the same campaign breakdown "structure."

The idea of having to figure out all the different pay-per-click (PPC) ad platforms out there probably feels overwhelming, right? I understand. You must pick two or three marketing strategies to execute on two or three ad platforms.

But I also wouldn't do that until I first set up a successful campaign on one platform. And what do I mean by success? It depends on your business objective for that campaign.

One of the problems that have cost me millions is the unproductive idea of multitasking. In the real business world, focus matters more than ideas. I find it cute when people talk about multitasking in this great light of new discoveries.

Many things are indeed happening at the same time in any given business. That's why I will have to put context as a priority over focus as well.

It all depends on what you mean. Each process among many in a system with respect to focus on a primary business objective has to be clearly defined if you don't want to waste resources. So it's best to set up a campaign successfully on one ad platform first and start collecting data before attempting to scale out to other platforms with the same "campaign breakdown structure."

If your business has less than 10 employees, I will cap out the number of ad platforms at three. The rest of the focus should go into the optimization of your campaigns on the two or three ad platforms you've chosen and your business operations.

Understanding a campaign breakdown structure is important because it's the same skeleton that you will implement on any platforms you choose to set up campaigns on. This "structure" will be useful from both a mental and a campaign execution standpoint. Once you understand it, you can successfully execute a digital marketing campaign on any ad platform.

Campaign Breakdown Structure

There are four levels of a digital marketing campaign breakdown structure. Each level allows you to define how you want your campaign to run.

Level 1 - How: The first level is simply defining the platform you choose to run it on.   This is the level where you decide which of the many ad platforms you want to run and test your PPC campaigns on. The rest of the levels are about the specifications inside the campaign itself.

Level 2 - Why: On this level, you get to choose the business objective of your campaign. What is the purpose of this campaign? The ultimate purpose of a digital marketing campaign is to make money, right? But you need to be a little more specific.

Is it to primarily generate the most video views, reach, visits to external pages, capture leads, or sales? When you are specific, it makes your desired outcome and results easier to track, measure, monitor, and control.

You may also be defining your budget for this campaign on this level.

Level 3 - Who: This is where you get to define your ideal prospect and/or customer and their attributes. It's very hard to be specific at this level, but you have to put in some effort for your digital marketing campaign.

At this level, you will get to define the following:

- Behavior-based on attributes known to the ad platform.
- The desired cost per result achieved.
- Location
- Age
- Gender
- Language

- Interest and followings

And more…

Level 4 - What: At this level is where you define the actual message that describes your offer to the audience you specified on level 3.

On the actual ad platform, you will get to upload the images, the video, and the ad copy, as we cover in more detail in Chapter 3, "the value."

This is the actual creative that the audience, again as defined on level 3, gets to see on the feed and the placements. So it needs to be intriguing enough to catch the attention of the audience you defined. Hence, I took the time to break down "the value" in chapter 3.

On Meta Ads (a.k.a Facebook Ads), levels 1,2, and 3 are Campaign, Ad sets, and Ads, respectively. On Google Ads, levels 1,2, and 3 are Campaign, Ad group, and Ads, respectively. I promise. On the other platforms that may be unconventional, it's similar.

At the end of this all, it's all in the mindset. Approach setting up a digital marketing campaign with these four level-structure, and your chances of a better outcome are sure.

Another way you can protect your business from losing money is to buy email marketing placement from other marketers who have built a healthy email list. Check out www.myEmpirePRO.com/traffic, especially if you are in the biz-opp or financial niche.

You can simply order clicks and visits over to your websites to pique initial interest. After that, you can then set up a retargeting or remarketing campaign on major platforms like Google Ads or Meta Ads to re-attract your audience from Facebook, Instagram, YouTube, Google, and their various media partners.

This is an unconventional way of driving consistent traffic and building your list. But you can still apply "the structure" mindset to stay organized. Anyway, in the next and final chapter, we will enter the execution zone, and it's time to put this wealth of knowledge to work.

THE CONCLUSION

In conclusion of this book *"Digital Marketing Certified,"* you will discover how to flip your thoughts & information into a $200,000+ per year income in 3 steps; no technical skills or experience are required.

And you will be able to do so without cold calling, texting strangers, pestering friends and family, knocking on doors, driving for dollars, and you don't even have to leave your house... ALL REMOTELY.

This is an opportunity for you to add a project to your resume that can actually pay a 6-figure income on the side.

I want to share a story of how I became responsible for the revenue of a little more than $3 million in 24 months and kept most of it doing exactly what I am about to show you.

You, too, can run a 6-7 figure business all from the comfort of anywhere you want on this planet with a laptop and internet connection by flipping your thoughts and information.

Who is this for?

1. Struggling Real Estate Wholesalers
2. Struggling Real Estate Agents
3. Struggling Agency Owners
4. Struggling Course Creators
5. Struggling MLM'er or Network Marketers
6. Struggling Internet Marketers & Funnel Builders
7. Struggling & Certified Professionals

It's a perfect program for stay-at-home moms, side hustlers, and the like.

Imagine waking up daily to email notifications of income ranging from $3 to $2,500 … in upwards of $200,000 per year on a 4-hour-per-week time budget.

Don't worry about the results. I'll show you how you can virtually GUARANTEE results for yourself, just like 1,000's of people that have gone through my teachings since 2009.

Creating a digital side hustle is very simple, and you can probably find free information all over the place:

- Google
- YouTube
- Facebook Groups
- Books
- Amazon

However, this level of accessibility has posed to become a problem because the internet is like a bathroom wall that everyone is throwing stuff on. So you don't even know who is telling the truth or not; everyone is a guru.

Nothing is worse than investing $25,000 into a coach you found at a hotel seminar or some random webinar only to find out that 1-2 years have passed, and you still haven't made a single penny, much less $200,000… even in 25 years.

You feel even worse if you've spent 40,000 hours watching free YouTube videos collecting information, doing every gimmicky thing prescribed by gurus such as:

- Cold-calling people who just curse at you
- Texting strangers,
- Pestering friends and family,
- Knocking on doors,

- Driving for dollars
- Selling cream and vitamins
- Calling yourself an entrepreneur…

Trying to become…

- Real Estate Wholesaler
- Real Estate Agent
- An Agency Owner
- A Course Creator
- An MLM'er or Network Marketer…Getting rejection with every interaction
- An Affiliate Marketer & Funnel Builder
- The Next Big Certified IT Professionals with 2 or 3 remote jobs

…Feeling like a dreamer and a failure to your family all at the same time. It's a terrible feeling. In this final chapter, I will help you stop all of that and put you on the right path.

There are 3 simple steps involved in flipping your thoughts into market value successfully but first, you should realize this. You are simply organizing your thoughts into an online journal.

After that, you can then use automated systems to attract people browsing and searching online who find value in your wisdom for up to a $15,000 fee. Your profit comes from the fact that you got here first.

I made $82,000, my highest net profit in one single day using the same method in real estate. So here is the "dirty" little secret of flipping your thoughts & information to money from anywhere.

Since 2005, I have been averaging as low as $3 and as high as $82,000 per sales commission deposited or wired directly into my business bank and PayPal accounts. Here are the 3 steps.

STEP 1 - Understanding that there is value in my experience, thoughts, and insights for other people.

STEP 2 - Leveraging automated systems to set up an online log of my daily thoughts and insights strategically aligned with products and services that people already want... up to $15,000 per customer.

STEP 3 - Attracting people and building an audience of people who are searching and browsing online for value into my online community.

Those are the 3 steps involved to start collecting some serious money consistently when you rinse and repeat. If you use a smartphone, a laptop, and social media, it's a simple digital age skill, and I will show you how to get it all setup and running within the next 11 days; we call it...

11 Days Challenge

But before that, who da heck am I, and how do I qualify to even talk about or present this $205,000 annual income formula and business opportunity to you?

My name is OLA. I am the creator of myEmpirePRO and the author of...

1. Digital Marketing Certified

2. Smart Real Estate Wholesaling

3. Real Estate Money Secrets

… and Get My Marriage Back, which I co-authored with my wife, Lola.

I launched my first profitable business back in 2005, and it was the last year of college when I bagged two seemingly useless degrees at the time from NJIT.

- B. Sc in Computer Engineering
- M. Sc in Engineering Management.

I learned the 40-40-40 plan from those 2 programs.

- Working 40 hours per week.
- For the next 40 years.
- Taking home $40,000 per year.

Wait… There is another "40". Trying to pay off a $40,000 school loan. The worst deal I have ever signed up for in my life.

Anyway, I joined the entrepreneurship game and closed my 1st deal in December 2005. I've closed tons of deals since then obviously while encountering 40,000+ obstacles.

But because of this opportunity, you don't have to experience the same obstacles and learning curve. Since the beginning, I've had $100, $1,000, $5,000, $15,000, and upwards of $82,000 in single days by simply flipping my thoughts, my insights, and information on the internet. But let's slow down.

After transactions worth over $3 million 2 years after my first deal, things started to slow down. I lost everything eventually. Thanks to the 2008 recession. Then I went on a mission to learn how to apply the Warren Buffett rule to the knowledge equity I had built from all the experience.

That Warren Buffet rule is to learn how to make money in my sleep, and the internet was a great place to learn that. Within one year, I was back to $40,000 per month in revenue without having to be on the streets or begging family and friends to do business with me.

In 2012, I applied the same modern-day marketing and business scaling skills to a partnership model, and it worked. But before I continue, it is important that I share this story with you, and you'll understand why in a minute.

*"Can I Make a Confession? **I don't enjoy taking risks.**"* And if you're like me and you'd prefer to do business without losing sleep at night on the fear of "what if" your life savings go south with big risks, we are on the same page.

For me, I only had 10 conditions before I could consider the risk low enough for me to take. So you will find in a second that building a digital 6-figure side hustle is not as risky or difficult as you may have thought.

What I wanted was:

1. To be able to do it from anywhere as long as I have my laptop and a decent internet connection,
2. A part-time 4 hours work-week just in case I need to maintain a full-time job temporarily.
3. To be able to secure at least a full-time 6-figure income doing it with a potential for 7-figure.
4. A business with no Equipment to manage
5. A business with no physical inventory to ship out to anybody.
6. A business with no employees must start and start making money.

7. A business with low upfront investment because I was coming out of college with no savings.
8. To be able to teach others because I know it would come back to me literally in multiple folds.
9. A business with no licenses, degrees or special certification was necessary because I wouldn't take out any more school loans anyway.
10. To Serve Basic Human Needs and be recession-proof essentially.

If you want an opportunity that would provide a decent lifestyle quickly and easily with something we all already engage in and even in this moment, then listen up closely.

Imagine being able to earn the money you need to Initiate the projects you are passionate about. Imagine becoming an investor for your loved ones' passion projects, being able to afford your desired charity initiative, being able to mess around and use cash to test other types of creative business ventures, and becoming an investor in the companies that create the products and services you use daily.

Isn't that the end goal, anyway? After hitting $10,000 in monthly residual income, I have been able to change my life and more because of the simple skills I will be revealing to you. It's all about attracting people while leveraging the year that we live in.

I call it 2000&DIGITAL.

My methods are very simple, and I use them to attract a minimum of 1,000 video views and 1,000+ hours of watch time every single day.

And by the way, my videos with 10-20 views tend to generate the most money because, at the end of the day, these are real human beings turning to daily income because of their value. I will show you how to set this all up easily.

So my offer to you is an 11 days challenge to follow my lead and get your thoughts and information-flipping empire all set up and running in 11 days.

If you have $9,875, you can make it happen to start today. So it would help if you, therefore, assumed that any price less than that on this page www.11DaysChallenge.com is for a limited time only.

You can take a RISK-FREE trial of the 11 Days Challenge. In 11 days, you will also be set up to do exactly the same thing that the gurus and top producers do effortlessly. Here is a breakdown of what to expect.

DAY 1 – Fundamentals & Overview

By the end of the first day, you will fully understand the fundamentals of flipping your thoughts and information into $200,000 in annual profits by way of my easy-to-understand teaching style.

DAY 2 – Branding YOU Inc. Formula

You would have picked the right name and set up a brand that positions you for high competitive advantage and brand equity.

DAY 3 – High Converting Bio Formula

You would have used our proprietary formula to set up two versions of bio that will get the best quality of prospects falling over each other to work with you.

DAY 4 – Social Media Branding Formula

You would have used our social media setup formula to set up profiles that will get the best quality of prospects falling over each other to work with you.

DAY 5 – Million Dollar Hub Formula

You would have set up your personal central information hub that is designed to log and flip its content to cash consistently.

DAY 6 – The System Formula

By the end of the 6th day, you would have used this formula, with my help, of course, to set up a machine that does all the selling for you. If you hate selling and bothering people to buy, this is a must-have part of your empire.

DAY 7 – The Invisible Money Formula

By the 7the day, you will learn how to build an online virtual bank that will potentially take care of you and your family for the rest of your life. I am aware that this is a bold statement.

DAY 8 – Self Liquidating Formula

Have you wondered, "exactly what am I going to be selling on the internet?". By the 8th day, that question will be answered. For now, just think about all those Amazon boxes that come to your doorstep on a monthly basis, damn near every day.

DAY 9 – The Research30 Library Formula

The foundational first 30 days of building a digital empire are very important, and one single mistake can mess it all up. With this formula, you would have eliminated one of the most terrible mistakes that many make when they don't have access to this challenge; winging things along.

DAY 10 – The Feed Formula

By the end of the 10th day, you would have successfully executed the feeding process of your digital empire for the first time.

DAY 11 – The Launch30 Library Formula

This includes a review of the last previous 10 days, a $5,000 value raffle draw & assessment. By the end of the last day of the challenge, you would have launched your very own digital information-flipping empire.

You will also be able to enter into a raffle draw to win $5,000 worth of additional value from our platform. And lastly, you will get an assessment to ensure that you are mastering the game of a profitable information-flipping digital empire from home.

Keep in mind that you don't have to do anything crazy like cold-calling people who just curse at you, texting strangers, pestering friends and family, knocking on doors, driving for dollars, selling cream and vitamins, and calling yourself an entrepreneur or a boss on social media. You can finally secure a 6-figure income business with this system.***

These are short 5 minutes, easy-to-navigate tutorials to get you up and running a 6 to 7-figure operation quickly and easily. I have created the 11 days challenge so that you can copy and paste my system that is working right now into your business and income template today.

If you are frustrated from looking for a simple-to-implement hustle from home, you need the 11 days challenge. But if you are looking for your 1st celebratory sale, even better simply because you don't have to unlearn 1983 old-school marketing strategies that don't work effectively and efficiently anymore.

This is the digital business empire exactly the way the gurus and biggest influencers do it. Life comes with very few guarantees, but here is one of them. Time will continue to pass, including the next 11 days.

And that's also whether or not we allow ourselves the pleasure and the adventure of building a million-dollar digital business empire within the next 11 days. If that sounds non-typical, that's normal, and the type of income and lifestyle you are contemplating on creating are non-typical.

But here is another guarantee. In addition to the low investment, you also have a 30 days 100% money-back guarantee. If any time before your 30th-day anniversary you feel that this isn't working for you, it's a one-click cancellation button, and you get 100% of your money back as long as it is within 30 days of that particular transaction. The only risk in your decision is attached to not taking action.

WARNING: Whatever price you are looking at on www.11DaysChallenge.com seems unrealistic, right? That's because it is unrealistically crazy. It's for a limited time only, and you will notice the countdown clock there...

What If You Are Already In A Business But Struggling?

99% are stuck on the guru's *"from grass to grace"* story, but they are going broke trying to implement it. There are so many wanna-be gurus teaching the old school and outdated ways or stuff they copied from a course repository. While the gurus are teaching these strategies that only work 1% of the time, they are growing influence and their marketing budget using strategies that work 100% of the time.

Remember that this 6-7 figures 11 days method and the system are 100% risk-free. I built the system we are using for myself, and it cost me $173,000, and it costs me a lot of money to maintain as well. You are not taking any risk… I am.

All you have to do is ride on my shoulders, and the years of experience I've built since closing my first deal in December 2005. Check it out at www.11DaysChallenge.com.

Here Are 4 Limited-Time Bonuses You Get Today When You Accept the 11 Days Challenge Today.

DMi15 - This is our Digital Marketing Intensive 15 Weeks Training. You will get to master the art and sciences of marketing and advertising in the digital age in 15 weeks and get certified.

(This is a $4,997 Value)

myEmpirePRO Inner Circle - By accepting this challenge, you are automatically accepted to join the inner circle for top-class and ongoing training support in your digital marketing career journey and endeavors.

(This is a $9,875 Value)

SUB-TOTAL BONUS VALUE: $14,872

myEmpirePRO Elite Coop Partnership - With this program, we accept a limited number of people to partner with us while we actually do all the work of building their digital business-empire feed.

(This is a $997 Value)

SUB-TOTAL BONUS VALUE: $15,869

11 Days Challenge to Wholesale Real Estate Operation - This is the 5 stages-execution of building your very own 6-7 figure wholesale real estate operation in the next 11 days.

(This is a $2,497 Value)

TOTAL BONUS VALUE: $18,366

In addition to the real-life testimonials and success stories you are about to watch here at www.11DaysChallenge.com , this is how we came up with a $200,000 potential annual income. We are not guaranteeing it since we can't guarantee your participation level over the next 11 days. But here it goes.

I will help you set up a system that collects $48.50 monthly from 100 customers, and that's $4,850 per month. The 11 days challenge is designed to help you set up a system that attracts prospects and, subsequently, the customers convert the sales by themselves.

Not only will the system attract customers, but it's also designed to help you build a team that will set up its own digital mini-franchise to attract its very own 100 customers.

You are entitled to 20% of that $48.50 they collect from each of these customers, and that's $9.70 each. So 100 customers of yours with 10 customers each or 10 customers of yours with their own 100 customers will result in 1,000 customers on the second level of your organization.

When you multiply that 1,000 customers by $9.70, that's a team production of $9,700. Go ahead and add that to your personal monthly production of $4,850. That's a total business revenue of $14,550; when you multiply that by 12 months, it's $174,600.

And then, there is the opportunity of upgrading 30% of your customers to a $ 1,000 sale for an additional $29,955 per year. We now have an estimated $2000,000 annual income, a bunch of relationships, a robust library of your thoughts based on the formula that has worked for us since 2009, and a bunch of professional relationships and partnerships that you can build more on; just for joining this powerful community.

Remember that this formula only assumes 10% success rate outside of your personal efforts and still pays lucratively. Watch this video from my friends who have used my training and systems to generate upwards of $230,000 per month and even $4 million in a single year.

I'll see you inside. www.11DaysChallenge.com

REFERENCES

The Countdown

Smart Real Estate Wholesaling by OLA

www.SmartRealEstateWholesaling.com

Real Estate Money Secrets by OLA

www.RealEstateMoneySecrets.com

Get My Marriage Back by LOLA & OLA

www.GetMyMarriageBack.com

One Thing by Gary Keller

www.myempirepro.com/onething

Watch This Book as Videos on YouTube.

www.myempirepro.com/dmc-on-youtube

WordPress Hosting

www.myEmpirePRO.com/hosting

Sales Funnels

www.myEmpirePRO.com/salesfunnel

ClickMagick

www.myEmpirePRO.com/clickmagick

Traffic on Demand

www.myEmpirePRO.com/traffic

11 Days Challenge

www.11DaysChallenge.com

NOTES

_____

_____

_____

_____

_____

_____

_____

_____

_____

_____

_____

NOTES

NOTES

Made in the USA
Middletown, DE
29 December 2022

18289895R00119